Great Taste ~ Low Fat

MEATLESS MAIN DISHES

TIME
LIFE
BOOKS

ALEXANDRIA, VIRGINIA

TABLE OF CONTENTS

Stuffed Cabbage with Dill Sauce

page 85

Italian Bread and Vegetable Salad

page 141

On the Grill

Salads

INTRODUCTION

Our mission at Great Taste~Low Fat is to take the work and worry out of everyday low-fat cooking; to provide delicious, fresh, and filling recipes for family and friends; to use quick, streamlined methods and available ingredients; and, within every recipe, to keep the percentage of calories from fat under 30 percent.

MEATLESS MAIN DISHES

In the past, the words "meatless" and "vegetarian" called to mind either a sparse serving of tofu and greens or a dense, bland casserole. But recent years have brought about a wonderful new generation of meatless cuisine. The inspiration for these colorful meals often comes from countries such as China and India, where the vegetarian way of life is, for large portions of the population, a centuries-old tradition. We're not suggesting you stop eating meat, poultry, and fish altogether. But you might want to serve a meatless meal once or twice a week; we believe you'll soon be doing it more often as you discover how tasty (and satisfying) meatless meals can be.

TIME FOR A CHANGE

Meatless meals are not just for "health-food nuts." In fact, they're a good idea for just about everyone. In its Dietary Guidelines for Americans, the USDA states that vegetarians who eat milk products and eggs enjoy excellent health, and that "you can get enough protein from a vegetarian diet as long as the variety and amounts of foods consumed are adequate." Our recipes include dairy products and eggs along with a wide assortment of grains, legumes, and vegetables to assure you of excellent nutrition—and delicious eating.

In the past, it was believed that people who ate no meat had to combine foods in a certain way to get enough protein. Protein is made up of building blocks called amino acids, and it's true that "complete" protein, which has all the amino acids in the correct proportions, is found only in foods from animal sources—and in soybeans, an important exception to the rule. But as long as you choose from a wide variety of foods over the course of a day, you'll get all the amino acids and protein you need. And a diet rich in vegetables, fruits, grains, and legumes assures you of a high intake of essential vitamins and minerals. Such a diet is also naturally low in fat.

THE MEATLESS "NEW WAVE"

Like many people, Sandy Gluck, our chef, went through a vegetarian phase when she was younger. "In those days, vegetarian recipes relied on high-fat ingredients to replace meat. Fake pâté was made from chopped nuts, and no casserole was complete without an inch of melted Cheddar on top. It wasn't exactly health food!" These days when Sandy serves her family a meatless meal—and she often does—the starting point is either a grain or produce that's at its peak. "I'll make grain-stuffed peppers in late summer, or design a dish around sweet potatoes and apples in winter."

Among the fruits of Sandy's creativity are some adaptations of dishes usually made with meat, poultry, or fish; others are meatless originals. In Soups & Stews, for example, you'll find Irish Barley Stew and Vegetable Tagine—versions of dishes ordinarily made with lamb. Skillet Dishes offers Sweet and Sour Vegetables minus the usual pork. Vegetarian Sloppy Joes, with their bold barbecue flavor, are based on beans rather than beef.

The chapter called Baked & Stuffed features such comforting favorites as Vegetable Pot Pie and Three-Pepper Pizza as well as Couscous-Stuffed Pepper Halves. On the Grill includes appetizing alternatives to steaks and burgers, from traditional Vegetable Shish Kebabs to Zucchini and Corn Tostadas baked on the grill. For the Salads chapter, Sandy has devised an international array of bountiful grain, bean, pasta, and vegetable salads, such as Pasta Marinara Salad, Mexican Salad with Salsa Vinaigrette, and Couscous Salad.

The Secrets section includes a recipe for a deeply flavorful Homemade Vegetable Broth that can be used in many of the main-dish recipes.

With such a wide variety of deliciously filling dishes to choose from, we're sure you'll enjoy these recipes—without missing anything!

CONTRIBUTING EDITORS

Sandra Rose Gluck, *a New York City chef, has years of experience creating delicious low-fat recipes that are quick to prepare. Her secret for satisfying results is to always aim for great taste and variety. By combining readily available, fresh ingredients with simple cooking techniques, Sandra has created the perfect recipes for today's busy lifestyles.*

Grace Young *has been the director of a major test kitchen specializing in low-fat and health-related cookbooks for over 12 years. Grace oversees the development, taste testing, and nutritional analysis of every recipe in Great Taste–Low Fat. Her goal is simple: take the work and worry out of low-fat cooking so that you can enjoy delicious, healthy meals every day.*

Kate Slate *has been a food editor for almost 20 years, and has published thousands of recipes in cookbooks and magazines. As the Editorial Director of Great Taste–Low Fat, Kate combined simple, easy to follow directions with practical low-fat cooking tips. The result is guaranteed to make your low-fat cooking as rewarding and fun as it is foolproof.*

NUTRITION

Every recipe in *Great Taste–Low Fat* provides per-serving values for the nutrients listed in the chart at right. The daily intakes listed in the chart are based on those recommended by the USDA and presume a nonsedentary lifestyle. The nutritional emphasis in this book is not only on controlling calories, but on reducing total fat grams. Research has shown that dietary fat metabolizes more easily into body fat than do carbohydrates and protein. In order to control the amount of fat in a given recipe and in your diet in general, no more than 30 percent of the calories should come from fat.

Nutrient	Women	Men
Fat	<65 g	<80 g
Calories	2000	2500
Saturated fat	<20 g	<25 g
Carbohydrate	300 g	375 g
Protein	50 g	65 g
Cholesterol	<300 mg	<300 mg
Sodium	<2400 mg	<2400 mg

These recommended daily intakes are averages used by the Food and Drug Administration and are consistent with the labeling on all food products. Although the values for cholesterol and sodium are the same for all adults, the other intake values vary depending on gender, ideal weight, and activity level. Check with a physician or nutritionist for your own daily intake values.

SECRETS OF LOW-FAT MEATLESS COOKING

MEATLESS MAIN DISHES

A meatless meal is much more than a dainty saucer of sprouts: Meals "minus meat" can be abundantly satisfying, as demonstrated by the hearty recipes in this book. These dishes feature substantial ingredients that are low in fat but pleasingly varied and intensely flavorful.

EASY, HEALTHFUL MEALS

The ingredients for meatless meals are mostly "ready-to-use" foods (for one thing, there's no boning or fat-trimming to be done!). Many of the foods profiled here are pantry staples that enable you to make a number of tasty meals without so much as a shopping trip.

• **Pasta and Breadstuffs:** Pasta is a mainstay of meatless meals; with so many sizes and shapes available, it's easy to keep things interesting. Linguine, penne, or broad noodles can be tossed with grilled or sautéed vegetables; couscous, a beadlike pasta shape, makes a fine filling for stuffed peppers. Any good brand of dried pasta, domestic or imported, will do. Vegetable pastas, which come in a range of reds, greens, and golds, are pretty, but offer no nutritional advantage: Spinach pasta, for instance, contains the equivalent of less than 1 tablespoon of spinach per cup of cooked pasta.

Bread also plays an important role in meatless meals. Crusty Italian bread adds body to soups and salads; corn or flour tortillas form the foundation for tacos, tostadas, and quesadillas. Middle Eastern pitas (pocket breads) can hold all sorts of fillings. For the sake of variety as well as better nutrition, choose whole-grain and multi-grain loaves as well as white breads; accompany meals with rolls, bread sticks, flatbreads, English muffins, or bagels. Breads can be frozen for 3 months: Double-wrap them so they don't dry out.

• **Rice, Grains, and Beans:** Long-grain white rice is a classic side dish, but don't overlook other grains as the basis for hearty meals. Brown rice has a nuttier, more robust flavor, but takes about 45 minutes to cook. (As a timesaver, bring the required amount of water to a boil and stir in the rice; cover, remove the pan from the heat, and refrigerate overnight. Presoaked brown rice will cook in about half the usual time; add more water if necessary.) Bulghur, a quick-cooking form of cracked wheat, makes a great salad; barley is wonderful in soups. Barley and white rice will keep for 1 year. Whole grains, such as bulghur and brown rice, are best kept in the freezer.

Keep your shelves stocked with several different types of canned beans, a convenient staple for meatless meals. You'll want to stock cans of kidney beans—both red and white—chick-peas, black beans, and pinto beans. Dried split peas and lentils cook more quickly than beans, so it's no bother to prepare them from scratch. Pick over and rinse dried legumes to remove any tiny pebbles or darkened or shriveled peas or lentils. Dried legumes will keep for a year or more, but they'll become even drier over time and may need longer cooking to soften them.

• **Starchy Vegetables:** Substantial soups, chowders, curries, and the like rely on starchy vegetables, usually roots or seeds. Potatoes—waxy small red ones as well as sweet potatoes—make thick, velvety puréed soups; big Idaho baking potatoes are almost a meal in themselves. Corn and peas are starchy but delicately sweet; both come in convenient frozen forms, although fresh can be substituted with a little extra effort.

• **Meaty Vegetables:** Their natural savory quality—considerably enhanced by cooking—makes ingredients such as eggplant and mushrooms welcome in vegetarian dishes, where they supply warm, hearty flavor. Eggplant takes on a lovely smoky taste when broiled, baked, or grilled; if not overcooked, it retains its slightly chewy texture. The familiar white button mushrooms are at their

continued on page 8

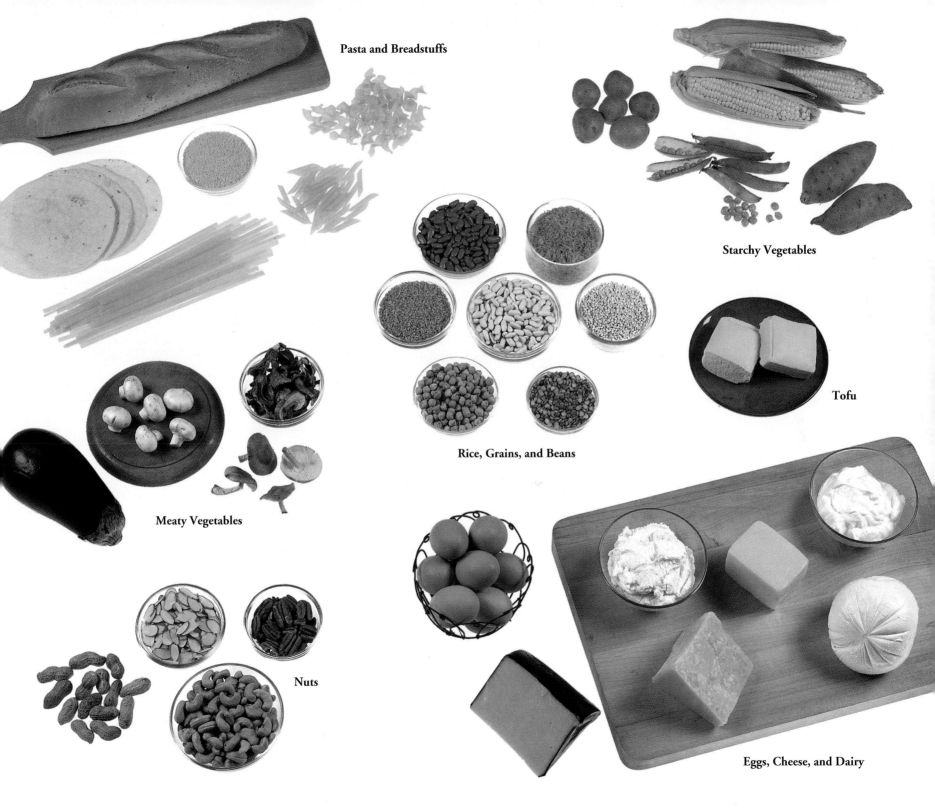

Pasta and Breadstuffs

Starchy Vegetables

Rice, Grains, and Beans

Tofu

Meaty Vegetables

Nuts

Eggs, Cheese, and Dairy

tastiest when grilled or sautéed; fresh shiitakes, a Japanese variety, are even more savory. For maximum flavor impact, turn to dried mushrooms: Italian porcini have a particularly rich flavor, but any dried mushrooms will do for our recipes.

• **Tofu:** Also called bean curd, this versatile soybean product comes in blocks that resemble ivory-colored cheese. Its texture, however, is more delicate than that of cheese—and tofu's neutral flavor can be seasoned in all sorts of ways. Surprisingly for a bean-based food, tofu derives more than 50 percent of its calories from fat. But most of the fat is unsaturated, and there is a "light" tofu available that has 75 percent less fat. Tofu is often sold in open tubs of water, which can be unsanitary: It's preferable to buy it in sealed packages. Store leftovers immersed in fresh water in a covered container; change the water daily. Tofu is available firm or soft. We use the firm type because it holds its shape when sliced or cubed. If necessary, firm up soft tofu this way: Sandwich the tofu between layers of paper towels, set it on a cutting board, and place a weight on top. Prop the cutting board at a slant so the excess liquid runs off, and let sit for about 30 minutes.

• **Eggs, Cheese, and Dairy:** With all the protein in grains, legumes, and vegetables, it's not necessary to add lots of eggs or cheese to meatless dishes. Whole eggs are fine as long as you don't eat them too often, but some recipes that use eggs can be made with egg whites alone (all the fat and cholesterol are in the yolks). When you do use cheese, stick to lower-fat types, such as part-skim ricotta and mozzarella, or use small amounts of sharper cheeses like Parmesan and Cheddar. Other dairy products come in lower-fat versions: reduced-fat sour cream; low-fat cottage cheese and yogurt; skim and 1% milk; and evaporated low-fat and skimmed milk.

• **Nuts:** Old-style vegetarian dishes often substituted nuts for meat. But nuts are high in fat, and should instead be used as a flavor and texture accent. Toasting enhances the flavor and crisps the nuts, too; it's easy to do and well worth the little time it takes. Because nuts are high in fat, they can become rancid. Store them in a sealed bag or other tightly closed container in the freezer.

VEGETABLE BROTH

Broth or stock is a basic ingredient of soups, stews, and sauces. The dishes in this book are made with vegetable broth rather than the usual chicken broth. You can buy canned vegetable broth in health-food shops and some supermarkets, but if you want to invest a little time, try this recipe for rich homemade broth. It's much less fussy to prepare than a meat or poultry stock, and much tastier than canned broth.

Homemade Vegetable Broth

There's lots of room for variation in this recipe. Feel free to substitute or add vegetables or herbs (but avoid very strongly flavored vegetables such as cabbage, broccoli, and Brussels sprouts). You can use vegetables that are a bit past their prime but not spoiled; slightly dried-up mushrooms add rich flavor.

Thickly slice 5 carrots and 3 ribs celery and place in a Dutch oven or large saucepan. Add 2 quartered, unpeeled onions, 6 cloves garlic (unpeeled), and a tomato, cut into chunks. Add 1 cup low-sodium tomato-vegetable juice and 8 cups water; bring to a boil over medium heat, skimming any foam that rises. Add ¼ cup parsley sprigs, 1 bay leaf (preferably Turkish), 1¼ teaspoons dried rosemary, ½ teaspoon dried thyme, ½ teaspoon salt, and ¼ teaspoon black pepper; partially cover and cook until the vegetables are very tender and the broth is richly flavored, about 1 hour. Strain and cool. Store the broth in the refrigerator for up to 1 week or freeze for up to 3 months. For convenience, freeze in 1-cup portions.   Makes 8 cups

SOUPS & STEWS

1

CARROT AND PARSNIP SOUP

SERVES: 4
WORKING TIME: 20 MINUTES
TOTAL TIME: 35 MINUTES

Taking a cue from French onion soup, we've partnered this earthy purée with cheese toasts, serving them alongside the soup rather than in it. The golden soup is a melding of potatoes, carrots, and parsnips, heightened with onion, garlic, tarragon, and orange zest. Evaporated skimmed milk adds creamy richness without adding any fat.

4 ounces French or Italian bread

½ cup shredded sharp Cheddar cheese (2 ounces)

2 teaspoons olive oil

1 onion, finely chopped

4 cloves garlic, minced

¾ pound all-purpose potatoes, peeled and thinly sliced

¾ pound parsnips, peeled and thinly sliced

3 carrots, thinly sliced

2 teaspoons sugar

1 teaspoon grated orange zest

¾ teaspoon dried tarragon

¼ teaspoon salt

¼ teaspoon freshly ground black pepper

2 cups reduced-sodium vegetable broth

1 cup evaporated skimmed milk

2 scallions, thinly sliced

1. Preheat the broiler. Slice the bread in half horizontally and place on a baking sheet. Sprinkle the Cheddar over the bread and broil until the cheese is melted, about 1 minute. Cut into 8 pieces.

2. Meanwhile, in a large saucepan, heat the oil until hot but not smoking over medium heat. Add the onion and garlic and cook, stirring, until the onion is softened, about 7 minutes. Add the potatoes, parsnips, and carrots. Sprinkle with the sugar, orange zest, tarragon, salt, and pepper, stirring to combine.

3. Add the broth and 1 cup of water to the pan and bring to a boil. Reduce to a simmer, cover, and cook until the vegetables are very tender, about 15 minutes. Transfer to a food processor and process to a smooth purée, about 1 minute. Return the soup to the saucepan, stir in the evaporated milk, and bring to a simmer. Divide the soup among 4 bowls and sprinkle the scallions over. Serve with the cheese toasts.

Helpful hint: Instead of transferring the vegetables to a food processor, you can use a hand blender right in the pot. Run the blender in on/off pulses until the soup is a smooth purée.

FAT: 8G/19%
CALORIES: 375
SATURATED FAT: 3.6G
CARBOHYDRATE: 61G
PROTEIN: 15G
CHOLESTEROL: 17MG
SODIUM: 627MG

IRISH BARLEY STEW

SERVES: 4
WORKING TIME: 20 MINUTES
TOTAL TIME: 35 MINUTES

There's usually lamb (or mutton) at the heart of an Irish barley stew, along with plenty of potatoes. Here, we've subtracted the meat and added lots more vegetables: Besides the potatoes there are carrots, parsnips, turnips, green beans, and peas. This adaptation will satisfy the heartiest appetites, especially if you serve a basket of warm rolls alongside.

1 tablespoon olive oil
2 carrots, cut into 1-inch lengths
2 parsnips, peeled and cut into 1-inch lengths
2 turnips, peeled and cut into 8 wedges each
½ pound small red potatoes, quartered
⅔ cup quick-cooking barley
¾ teaspoon salt
½ teaspoon dried thyme
¼ teaspoon freshly ground black pepper
¾ pound green beans, cut into 1-inch lengths
1 cup frozen peas

1. In a large saucepan, heat the oil until hot but not smoking over medium heat. Add the carrots, parsnips, and turnips and cook, stirring frequently, until lightly browned, about 5 minutes. Add the potatoes, barley, salt, thyme, and pepper, stirring to coat. Add 3⅓ cups of water and bring to a boil. Reduce to a simmer, cover, and cook until the vegetables and barley are tender, about 10 minutes.

2. Stir the green beans into the pan, cover, and cook until the green beans are crisp-tender, about 5 minutes. Add the peas and cook, uncovered, until heated through, about 2 minutes.

Helpful hint: Quick-cooking barley, which has been precooked by steaming, is ready in less than 15 minutes, while regular pearl barley takes nearly an hour to cook.

FAT: 4G/12%
CALORIES: 299
SATURATED FAT: 0.5G
CARBOHYDRATE: 59G
PROTEIN: 9G
CHOLESTEROL: 0MG
SODIUM: 523MG

A light Italian-style soup of spinach cooked in broth—"in brodo"—becomes a filling main dish with the addition of potatoes and chick-peas. Legumes, such as beans, chick-peas, and split peas, are excellent low-fat protein sources, making them both healthful and satisfying substitutes for meat and poultry.

CHICK-PEA AND SPINACH SOUP

SERVES: 4
WORKING TIME: 20 MINUTES
TOTAL TIME: 30 MINUTES

1 tablespoon olive oil

1 onion, finely chopped

6 cloves garlic, minced

2 carrots, halved lengthwise and thinly sliced

¾ pound all-purpose potatoes, peeled and cut into ½-inch cubes

2 cups reduced-sodium vegetable broth

16-ounce can chick-peas, rinsed and drained

½ teaspoon salt

½ teaspoon grated lemon zest

¼ teaspoon freshly ground black pepper

10-ounce package fresh spinach, shredded (see tip)

1. In a large nonstick saucepan, heat the oil until hot but not smoking over medium heat. Add the onion and garlic and cook, stirring frequently, until the onion is softened, about 7 minutes. Add the carrots and cook, stirring, until the carrots are crisp-tender, about 3 minutes.

2. Add the potatoes to the pan, stirring to coat. Add the broth, 1 cup of water, the chick-peas, salt, lemon zest, and pepper and bring to a boil. Reduce to a simmer, cover, and cook until the potatoes are firm-tender, about 7 minutes. Stir in the spinach and cook for 1 minute to wilt. Divide among 4 bowls and serve.

Helpful hint: There are three basic types of spinach. Savoy is the crinkly-leaf spinach usually sold pre-washed in bags. There are also semi-Savoy (less crinkly) and smooth-leaved types. Any of the three can be used in this recipe.

The easiest way to shred spinach or other broad-leaved greens is to stack the leaves and then slice them crosswise.

FAT: 6G/23%
CALORIES: 233
SATURATED FAT: 0.6G
CARBOHYDRATE: 38G
PROTEIN: 10G
CHOLESTEROL: 0MG
SODIUM: 604MG

VEGETABLE-BEAN SOUP

SERVES: 4
WORKING TIME: 25 MINUTES
TOTAL TIME: 30 MINUTES

1 tablespoon olive oil

4 cloves garlic, minced

1 tablespoon finely chopped fresh ginger

1 red bell pepper, cut into 1-inch squares

1 green bell pepper, cut into 1-inch squares

1 Granny Smith apple, cored, peeled, and cut into ½-inch cubes

2 teaspoons paprika

½ teaspoon salt

2 tomatoes, coarsely chopped, or 2 cups canned no-salt-added tomatoes, chopped with their juices

¾ pound green beans, cut into 1-inch lengths

16-ounce can red kidney beans, rinsed and drained

2 tablespoons balsamic vinegar

1. In a large saucepan, heat the oil until hot but not smoking over medium heat. Add the garlic and ginger and cook, stirring frequently, until the garlic is softened, about 1 minute. Add the bell peppers and cook, stirring frequently, until the peppers are crisp-tender, about 5 minutes. Add the apple, paprika, and salt and cook, stirring frequently, until the apple is crisp-tender, about 4 minutes.

2. Add 4 cups of water, the tomatoes, green beans, and kidney beans to the pan and bring to a boil. Reduce to a simmer, cover, and cook until the green beans are crisp-tender, about 5 minutes. Stir in the vinegar and serve.

Helpful hint: Green and red bell peppers differ not just in color, but in flavor: Red peppers have been left on the vine longer than green, and are therefore sweeter.

FAT: 5G/23%
CALORIES: 196
SATURATED FAT: 0.6G
CARBOHYDRATE: 33G
PROTEIN: 9G
CHOLESTEROL: 0MG
SODIUM: 429MG

Adding beans to just about any meatless soup makes a more satisfying meal. Here, the kidney beans contribute starchy sturdiness and protein, while green beans, bell peppers, and apple cubes bring a fresh, crisp quality to the soup. The lively finishing touch is a splash of vinegar; mellow balsamic works particularly well, but red wine vinegar could be used instead.

CURRIED SPLIT PEAS OVER RICE

SERVES: 4
WORKING TIME: 20 MINUTES
TOTAL TIME: 50 MINUTES

Indian meals frequently revolve around soup-like dishes made from lentils or split peas, known as "dals." There's something wonderfully homey and soothing about the combination of a dal and rice; here, the flavors of garlic, fennel, curry, coriander, and cumin make for a richly savory dish. Top the yogurt sauce with a sprinkling of chopped fresh parsley or basil, if you like.

1 cup long-grain rice
¾ teaspoon salt
1 cup plain nonfat yogurt
2 teaspoons curry powder
1¼ teaspoons ground coriander
1¼ teaspoons ground cumin
3 tablespoons olive oil
2 cups frozen pearl onions
1 red bell pepper, cut into ½-inch squares
3 cloves garlic, minced
¾ teaspoon fennel seeds, crushed
¾ pound small red potatoes, cut into ½-inch chunks
1 cup split peas, rinsed and picked over
1 cup canned no-salt-added tomatoes, chopped with their juices
1 cup frozen peas

1. In a medium saucepan, bring 2¼ cups of water to a boil. Add the rice and ¼ teaspoon of the salt, reduce to a simmer, cover, and cook until the rice is tender, about 17 minutes.

2. Meanwhile, in a small bowl, combine the yogurt, ½ teaspoon of the curry powder, ¼ teaspoon of the coriander, and ¼ teaspoon of the cumin. Refrigerate until serving time.

3. In a large saucepan, heat the oil until hot but not smoking over medium-high heat. Add the onions and bell pepper and cook, stirring frequently, until the pepper is crisp-tender, about 5 minutes. Reduce the heat to medium, add the garlic, and cook, stirring frequently, for 1 minute. Add the fennel, the remaining 1½ teaspoons curry powder, the remaining 1 teaspoon each coriander and cumin, and the remaining ½ teaspoon salt. Cook, stirring, until well coated, about 1 minute.

4. Add the potatoes, split peas, and tomatoes to the pan, stirring to combine. Add 2¾ cups of water and bring to a boil. Reduce to a simmer, cover, and cook until the split peas are tender, about 30 minutes. Stir in the frozen peas and cook until just heated through, about 2 minutes. Divide the rice among 4 bowls and spoon the split pea mixture over. Top with a dollop of the yogurt mixture and serve.

FAT: 12G/18%
CALORIES: 616
SATURATED FAT: 1.6G
CARBOHYDRATE: 105G
PROTEIN: 24G
CHOLESTEROL: 1MG
SODIUM: 531MG

VEGETABLE STEW WITH SPICY PEANUT SAUCE

SERVES: 4
WORKING TIME: 20 MINUTES
TOTAL TIME: 35 MINUTES

Peanuts are little more than a snack food for Americans, but in Africa, these versatile legumes are used to enrich soups and sauces, and as a meat substitute. This peanut-sauced stew is reminiscent of an African recipe usually made with chicken; we've filled the pot with a pleasing variety of vegetables instead. You'll love the contrast of nutty-sweet peanut butter and hot chilies.

2 teaspoons olive oil
1 onion, finely chopped
4 cloves garlic, minced
1 pickled jalapeño pepper, finely chopped
2 green bell peppers, cut into 1-inch squares
1 red bell pepper, cut into 1-inch squares
2 zucchini, halved lengthwise and cut into 1-inch pieces
¾ pound all-purpose potatoes, peeled and cut into ½-inch cubes
¾ pound sweet potatoes, peeled and cut into ½-inch cubes
1½ cups reduced-sodium vegetable broth
¾ teaspoon ground ginger
½ teaspoon salt
¼ teaspoon cayenne pepper
8-ounce can no-salt-added tomato sauce
1 tablespoon creamy peanut butter

1. In a large saucepan, heat the oil until hot but not smoking over medium heat. Add the onion, garlic, and jalapeño and cook, stirring frequently, until the onion is softened, about 7 minutes. Add the bell peppers and zucchini and cook, stirring frequently, until the bell peppers are crisp-tender, about 5 minutes.

2. Add the all-purpose potatoes, sweet potatoes, broth, ginger, salt, and cayenne to the pan and bring to a boil. Reduce to a simmer, cover, and cook until the potatoes are tender, about 10 minutes. Stir in the tomato sauce and peanut butter and bring to a boil. Reduce to a simmer, cover, and cook until the stew is richly flavored, about 5 minutes.

Helpful hint: This is a good candidate for make-ahead: Prepare the soup the day before, being careful not to overcook it. Then reheat it slowly over medium heat, adding a little broth or water if it is too dry.

FAT: 5G/18%
CALORIES: 246
SATURATED FAT: 0.7G
CARBOHYDRATE: 46G
PROTEIN: 8G
CHOLESTEROL: 0MG
SODIUM: 471MG

Lentil and Cauliflower Stew

Serves: 4
Working time: 25 minutes
Total time: 45 minutes

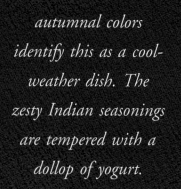

Its *autumnal colors identify this as a cool-weather dish. The zesty Indian seasonings are tempered with a dollop of yogurt.*

1 cup long-grain rice
¾ teaspoon salt
1 tablespoon olive oil
1 onion, finely chopped
4 cloves garlic, minced
2 carrots, thinly sliced
1 cup lentils, rinsed and picked over
¾ pound plum tomatoes, coarsely chopped, or 1½ cups no-salt-added canned tomatoes, chopped with their juices
2 cups reduced-sodium vegetable broth
1 teaspoon ground ginger
½ teaspoon ground coriander
⅛ teaspoon ground allspice
4 cups cauliflower florets
1 cup plain nonfat yogurt

1. In a medium saucepan, bring 2¼ cups of water to a boil. Add the rice and ¼ teaspoon of the salt, reduce to a simmer, cover, and cook until the rice is tender, about 17 minutes.

2. Meanwhile, in a large nonstick saucepan, heat the oil until hot but not smoking over medium heat. Add the onion and garlic and cook, stirring occasionally, until the onion is softened, about 7 minutes. Add the carrots and cook, stirring occasionally, until the carrots are crisp-tender, about 4 minutes.

3. Add the lentils to the pan, stirring to coat. Add the tomatoes, broth, ginger, coriander, allspice, and the remaining ½ teaspoon salt and bring to a boil. Reduce to a simmer, cover, and cook until the lentils have begun to soften, about 10 minutes. Stir in the cauliflower, cover, and cook until the lentils and cauliflower are tender, about 10 minutes. Divide the rice among 4 bowls. Spoon the stew alongside, top with a dollop of the yogurt, and serve.

Helpful hint: If properly cooked, lentils will hold their shape and still be slightly firm. If simmered too long, they will dissolve into mush, so time the cooking carefully.

Fat: 5g/9%
Calories: 494
Saturated Fat: 0.8g
Carbohydrate: 90g
Protein: 25g
Cholesterol: 1mg
Sodium: 630mg

CREAM OF BROCCOLI SOUP

Serves: 4
Working time: 30 minutes
Total time: 40 minutes

2 teaspoons olive oil

1 onion, finely chopped

3 cloves garlic, minced

1¼ pounds broccoli

1 pound all-purpose potatoes, peeled and thinly sliced

2½ cups reduced-sodium vegetable broth

¾ teaspoon dried marjoram

½ teaspoon salt

¼ teaspoon freshly ground black pepper

1 cup evaporated skimmed milk

⅛ teaspoon cayenne pepper

2 tablespoons reduced-fat sour cream

2 teaspoons flour

½ cup shredded Cheddar cheese (2 ounces)

1. In a nonstick Dutch oven, heat the oil until hot but not smoking over medium heat. Add the onion and garlic and cook, stirring frequently, until the onion is softened, about 7 minutes.

2. Meanwhile, with a paring knife, separate the broccoli florets and stems; peel the stems and thinly slice them.

3. Add the potatoes to the pan, stirring well to combine. Add the broccoli stems and all but 1 cup of the broccoli florets, stirring to combine. Add the broth, 1 cup of water, the marjoram, salt, and pepper and bring to a boil. Reduce to a simmer, cover, and cook until the potatoes and broccoli stems are tender, about 12 minutes. Meanwhile, in a small pot of boiling water, cook the reserved cup of broccoli florets for 2 minutes to blanch. Drain.

4. Transfer the vegetable mixture to a food processor and process to a smooth purée. Return the soup to the pan, stir in the evaporated milk and cayenne, and bring to a simmer. In a small bowl, stir together the sour cream and flour. Add the sour cream mixture and blanched broccoli florets to the pan and cook, stirring, until slightly thickened, about 1 minute. Divide the soup among 4 bowls, sprinkle the Cheddar over, and serve.

Helpful hint: Adding flour to the sour cream helps keep it from curdling when added to the hot soup.

Fat: 9g/29%
Calories: 279
Saturated Fat: 3.9g
Carbohydrate: 37g
Protein: 16g
Cholesterol: 20mg
Sodium: 636mg

With a few minor adjustments, we've transformed this classic cheese-topped "cream" soup into healthy fare.

ITALIAN BREAD SOUP

SERVES: 4
WORKING TIME: 40 MINUTES
TOTAL TIME: 55 MINUTES

Making use of leftover bread was no doubt the inspiration for classic country-style bread soup. We call for fresh bread, however, and toast the slices to dry them out a bit. The toasts are topped with Parmesan and are submerged in an oniony vegetable soup, which is then baked to blend the marvelous flavors. A simple salad is all you need to add for a delicious, hearty supper.

4 ounces French or Italian bread, cut into ½-inch-thick slices

⅓ cup grated Parmesan cheese

1 tablespoon olive oil

2 leeks or 4 scallions, thinly sliced

1 onion, finely chopped

6 cloves garlic, minced

2 carrots, thinly sliced

2 ribs celery, thinly sliced

1 red bell pepper, cut into ½-inch squares

4 cups shredded cabbage

1 cup chopped plum tomatoes, or 1 cup no-salt-added canned tomatoes, chopped with their juices

1 cup canned white kidney beans (cannellini), rinsed and drained

2 cups reduced-sodium vegetable broth

½ teaspoon salt

½ teaspoon dried rosemary

1. Preheat the oven to 350°. Place the bread on a baking sheet and toast for 4 minutes per side or until lightly browned. Sprinkle the Parmesan over the toast and continue toasting for 4 minutes, or until the cheese is melted. Leave the oven on.

2. Meanwhile, in a nonstick Dutch oven or casserole, heat the oil until hot but not smoking over medium heat. Add the leeks, onion, and garlic and cook, stirring frequently, until the onion is softened, about 7 minutes. Add the carrots, celery, and bell pepper and cook, stirring frequently, until the carrots are crisp-tender, about 4 minutes.

3. Add the cabbage to the pan, stir to coat, cover, and cook until the cabbage is wilted, about 5 minutes. Add the tomatoes, beans, broth, salt, rosemary, and 4 cups of water and bring to a boil. Add the cheese toasts to the pot, lifting up the vegetable mixture so that the bread is buried. Cover, transfer to the oven, and bake until the soup is rich and flavorful, about 15 minutes. Divide the soup among 4 bowls and serve.

Helpful hint: Rosemary is often used in Italian bean-and-vegetable dishes, but if it's not to your taste, try oregano or thyme.

FAT: 7G/20%
CALORIES: 315
SATURATED FAT: 2G
CARBOHYDRATE: 51G
PROTEIN: 14G
CHOLESTEROL: 5MG
SODIUM: 840MG

CREAMY VEGETABLE STEW

SERVES: 4
WORKING TIME: 35 MINUTES
TOTAL TIME: 50 MINUTES

1 cup long-grain rice

¾ teaspoon salt

2 teaspoons olive oil

*1 red onion, cut into
1-inch chunks*

6 cloves garlic, peeled and halved

*2 red bell peppers, cut into
1-inch squares*

*¾ pound all-purpose potatoes,
peeled and cut into ½-inch
chunks*

*½ pound sweet potatoes, peeled
and cut into ½-inch chunks*

½ teaspoon dried marjoram

*¼ teaspoon freshly ground black
pepper*

*½ pound green beans, cut into
1-inch lengths*

1 cup evaporated low-fat milk

1 cup frozen peas

⅓ cup grated Parmesan cheese

1. In a medium saucepan, bring 2¼ cups of water to a boil. Add the rice and ¼ teaspoon of the salt, reduce to a simmer, cover, and cook until the rice is tender, about 17 minutes.

2. Meanwhile, in a medium saucepan, heat the oil until hot but not smoking over medium heat. Add the onion and garlic and cook, stirring frequently, until the onion is softened, about 5 minutes. Add the bell peppers and cook, stirring frequently, until the peppers are crisp-tender, about 5 minutes.

3. Add the all-purpose potatoes, sweet potatoes, marjoram, black pepper, the remaining ½ teaspoon salt, and 2 cups of water to the pan. Bring to a boil, reduce to a simmer, cover, and cook until the potatoes are tender, about 10 minutes. Add the green beans, cover, and cook until the green beans are almost tender, about 3 minutes.

4. Add the evaporated milk and peas and cook, stirring frequently, until the beans are tender and the sauce is slightly thickened, about 4 minutes. Divide the rice among 4 plates. Spoon the stew alongside the rice, top with the Parmesan, and serve.

Helpful hints: Evaporated low-fat milk has 6 grams of fat per cup, compared with 90 grams of fat for the same amount of heavy cream. If evaporated low-fat milk isn't available, substitute evaporated skimmed milk.

FAT: 6G/12%
CALORIES: 451
SATURATED FAT: 1.7G
CARBOHYDRATE: 84G
PROTEIN: 17G
CHOLESTEROL: 15MG
SODIUM: 668MG

A creamy sauce and a cheese topping make this a particularly enticing entrée. The garlic-and-marjoram-scented sauce surrounds sweet and all-purpose potatoes, red onion, bell peppers, green beans, and peas. Six cloves of garlic sounds like a lot, but after simmering, the garlic flavor is considerably mellowed. As a change from rice, serve the stew with wide noodles.

MOROCCAN VEGETABLE SOUP

SERVES: 4
WORKING TIME: 30 MINUTES
TOTAL TIME: 1 HOUR

The earthy hues of this soup hint at its rich, savory flavors. Pungent red and gold spices— paprika, coriander, cumin, and ginger— suffuse the vegetables, lentils, and chick-peas. Legumes, including beans, lentils, chick-peas, and split peas, are satisfying meat substitutes.

1 tablespoon olive oil

1 onion, finely chopped

2 carrots, halved lengthwise and thinly sliced

2 ribs celery, thinly sliced

1⅓ cups lentils, rinsed and picked over

1 tomato, coarsely chopped, or 1 cup no-salt-added canned tomatoes, chopped with their juices

1 cup low-sodium tomato-vegetable juice

2 teaspoons paprika

1½ teaspoons ground coriander

1½ teaspoons ground cumin

1 teaspoon ground ginger

¾ teaspoon salt

½ teaspoon freshly ground black pepper

19-ounce can chick-peas, rinsed and drained

2 tablespoons fresh lemon juice

1. In a large saucepan, heat the oil until hot but not smoking over medium heat. Add the onion and cook, stirring frequently, until tender, about 7 minutes. Add the carrots and celery and cook, stirring frequently, until the carrots are crisp-tender, about 5 minutes.

2. Add the lentils, tomato, tomato-vegetable juice, paprika, coriander, cumin, ginger, salt, and pepper to the pan, stirring to coat. Add 6 cups of water and bring to a boil. Reduce to a simmer, cover, and cook for 15 minutes. Add the chick-peas and cook, stirring occasionally, until the lentils are tender, about 15 minutes. Stir in the lemon juice. Divide among 4 bowls and serve.

Helpful hints: If you make the soup a day ahead of time, the flavors will mellow and blend beautifully; add the lemon juice just before serving, though.

FAT: 7G/15%
CALORIES: 416
SATURATED FAT: 0.7G
CARBOHYDRATE: 67G
PROTEIN: 25G
CHOLESTEROL: 0MG
SODIUM: 653MG

Okra, corn, and tomatoes make a classic Southern combination that you can enjoy at any time of year, thanks to the excellent quality of frozen okra and frozen corn kernels. We've rounded out the dish with lima beans and pasta, and dressed it up a bit with herbs and Parmesan.

SOUTHERN-STYLE VEGETABLE AND PASTA STEW

SERVES: 4
WORKING TIME: 25 MINUTES
TOTAL TIME: 35 MINUTES

6 ounces small pasta shells or elbow macaroni

1 tablespoon olive oil

1 onion, finely chopped

4 cloves garlic, minced

10-ounce package frozen baby lima beans, thawed

10-ounce package frozen cut okra (see tip), thawed

14½-ounce can no-salt-added stewed tomatoes, chopped with their juices

½ teaspoon salt

½ teaspoon dried rosemary

¼ teaspoon dried thyme

¼ teaspoon cayenne pepper

1 cup frozen corn kernels

½ cup grated Parmesan cheese

⅓ cup chopped fresh parsley

1. In a large pot of boiling water, cook the pasta until tender. Drain well.

2. Meanwhile, in a medium saucepan, heat the oil until hot but not smoking over medium heat. Add the onion and garlic and cook, stirring frequently, until the onion is softened, about 7 minutes. Add the lima beans and okra and cook, stirring frequently, until heated through, about 5 minutes.

3. Stir the tomatoes, salt, rosemary, thyme, and cayenne into the pan and bring to a boil. Reduce to a simmer, cover, and cook until the vegetables are tender, about 10 minutes. Stir in the corn and cook until heated through, about 3 minutes. Stir in the Parmesan and parsley. Combine with the pasta, divide among 4 bowls, and serve.

Helpful hint: Fresh corn kernels, cut from the cob, could be used in this recipe. You'll need 2 medium ears of corn to yield 1 cup of kernels.

FAT: 8G/17%
CALORIES: 433
SATURATED FAT: 2.6G
CARBOHYDRATE: 74G
PROTEIN: 19G
CHOLESTEROL: 8MG
SODIUM: 520MG

TIP

Okra is a finger-sized, tapered green pod vegetable with a flavor reminiscent of asparagus. When cooked in liquid, okra acts as a thickener, adding body with no extra fat. It's a favorite in Southern cooking, especially for gumbos. You can use fresh okra for this recipe, if you like. Choose plump, firm, bright green pods no more than 3 inches long and store in the refrigerator, unwashed, for up to 2 days. Cut the pods into ¾-inch-thick slices.

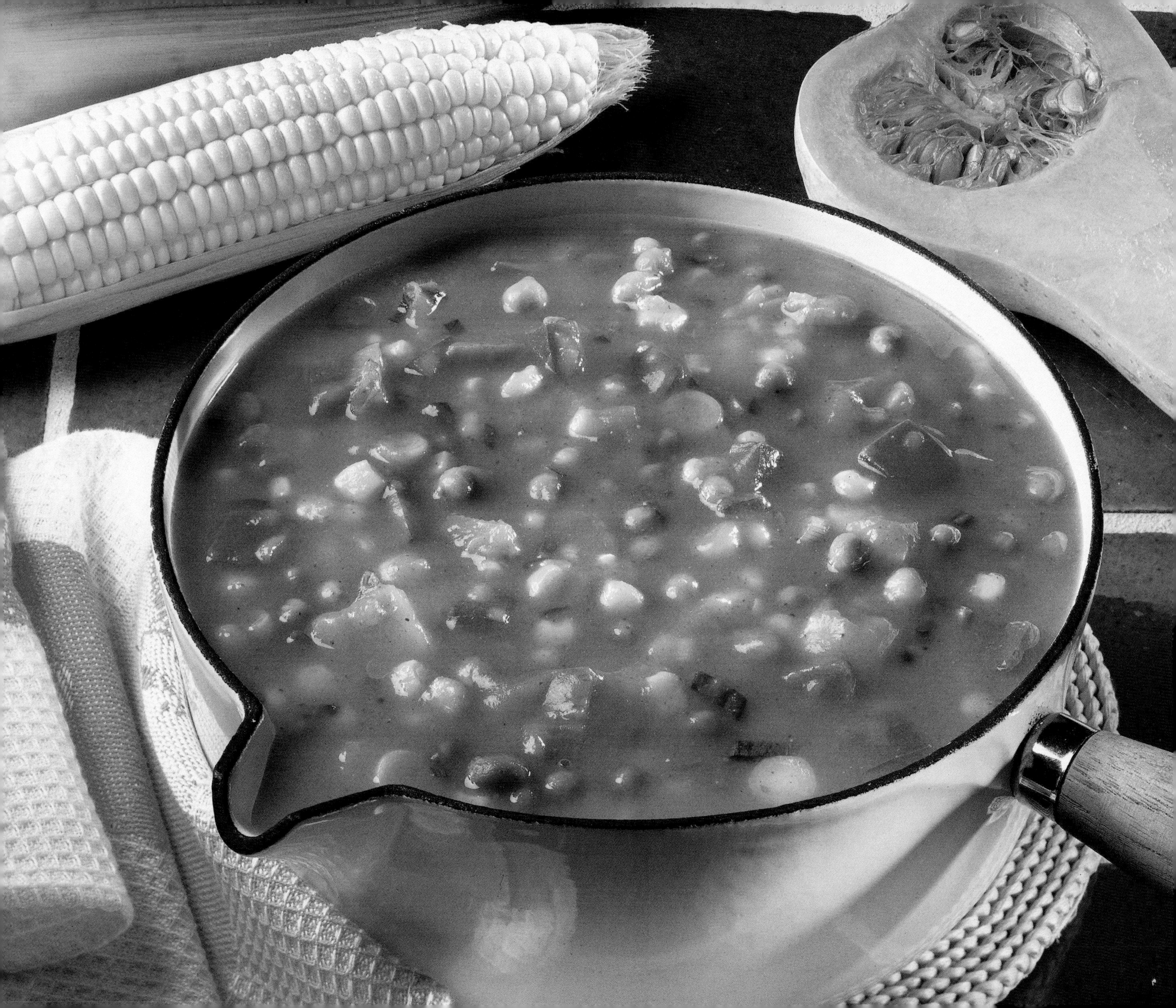

WINTER SQUASH AND CORN CHOWDER

SERVES: 4
WORKING TIME: 25 MINUTES
TOTAL TIME: 40 MINUTES

We generally think of chowders as being made with fish or seafood, but you can simmer up a thick, satisfying chowder with vegetables alone. Winter squash in a most convenient form—a frozen purée—gets this meal off to a quick start. Accompany the chowder with some saltines or oyster crackers, if you like.

½ pound all-purpose potatoes, peeled and cut into ½-inch cubes

1 tablespoon olive oil

6 scallions, thinly sliced

1 red bell pepper, cut into ¼-inch dice

1 green bell pepper, cut into ¼-inch dice

Two 10-ounce packages frozen puréed winter squash, thawed

1½ cups reduced-sodium vegetable broth

2 teaspoons sugar

2 teaspoons chili powder

1 teaspoon ground cumin

¾ teaspoon salt

1 cup frozen corn kernels

1 cup frozen peas

2 tablespoons fresh lime juice

1. In a medium pot of boiling water, cook the potatoes until tender, about 5 minutes. Drain.

2. In a medium saucepan, heat the oil until hot but not smoking over medium heat. Add the scallions and cook, stirring frequently, until softened, about 1 minute. Add the bell peppers and cook, stirring frequently, until the peppers are tender, about 5 minutes.

3. Stir the winter squash, broth, 1 cup of water, the sugar, chili powder, cumin, and salt into the pan and bring to a boil. Reduce to a simmer, cover, and cook until rich and flavorful, about 5 minutes. Stir in the potatoes, corn, and peas and cook until heated through, about 2 minutes. Stir in the lime juice and serve.

Helpful hint: To thaw the frozen squash in a microwave, remove the squash from the package and place in a microwave-safe bowl. Defrost on low power for 5 minutes.

FAT: 4G/15%
CALORIES: 249
SATURATED FAT: 0.5G
CARBOHYDRATE: 50G
PROTEIN: 8G
CHOLESTEROL: 0MG
SODIUM: 571MG

Spiced Sweet Potato Soup

SERVES: 4
WORKING TIME: 30 MINUTES
TOTAL TIME: 50 MINUTES

1 tablespoon olive oil

Two 6-inch corn tortillas, cut into ½-inch-wide strips

1 green bell pepper, cut into thin strips

1 red bell pepper, cut into thin strips

6 scallions, thinly sliced

1 pickled jalapeño pepper, finely chopped

1¼ pounds sweet potatoes, peeled and thinly sliced

¼ cup long-grain rice

2 cups reduced-sodium vegetable broth

¼ cup chili sauce

½ teaspoon grated lime zest

¼ cup fresh lime juice

¼ teaspoon salt

1 cup evaporated low-fat milk

½ cup shredded Monterey jack cheese (2 ounces)

1. In a large saucepan, heat the oil until hot but not smoking over medium heat. Add the tortillas and cook, turning them, until lightly crisped, about 2 minutes. With a slotted spoon, transfer the tortilla strips to paper towels.

2. Set aside ¼ cup each of the green and red bell pepper strips. Add the remaining bell pepper strips, the scallions, and jalapeño pepper to the saucepan and cook, stirring frequently, until the peppers are tender, about 5 minutes. Add the sweet potatoes and rice, stirring to combine. Add the broth, 1 cup of water, the chili sauce, lime zest, 2 tablespoons of the lime juice, and the salt and bring to a boil. Reduce to a simmer, cover, and cook until the potatoes and rice are tender, about 17 minutes. Meanwhile, in a small pot of boiling water, cook the reserved bell pepper strips for 1 minute to blanch. Drain. When cool enough to handle, dice the peppers.

3. Transfer the soup to a food processor and process to a smooth purée. Return the soup to the pan, stir in the evaporated milk, and bring to a simmer. Stir in the remaining 2 tablespoons lime juice. Divide the soup among 4 bowls. Sprinkle with the tortilla strips, diced bell peppers, and jack cheese, and serve.

Helpful hint: Instead of transferring the vegetables to a food processor, you can use a hand blender right in the pot. Run the blender in on/off pulses until the soup is a smooth purée.

FAT: 10G/25%
CALORIES: 364
SATURATED FAT: 3.1G
CARBOHYDRATE: 58G
PROTEIN: 13G
CHOLESTEROL: 25MG
SODIUM: 728MG

The confetti-like garnish that tops this puréed soup consists of bell peppers, tortilla strips, and jack cheese. And despite the suave, velvety appearance of the soup itself, there's plenty of spicy excitement going on beneath the surface: The potato-rice purée is laced with jalapeño, chili sauce, and lime. Serve the soup with warmed tortillas or crisp breadsticks.

Vegetable Tagine

A Moroccan tagine is a complex vegetable stew usually made with lamb, beef, or, perhaps, chicken. But the intriguing seasonings of a tagine work beautifully in an all-vegetable context, too.

There is also a wonderful interplay of ingredients: The prunes accentuate the subtle sweetness of the carrots, while the almonds bring out the nutlike flavor of the chick-peas.

1 tablespoon olive oil

1 onion, cut into ½-inch chunks

3 cloves garlic, minced

1 pound small red potatoes, cut into ½-inch chunks

1 teaspoon ground cumin

1 teaspoon paprika

¾ teaspoon ground ginger

¾ teaspoon salt

2 carrots, halved lengthwise and cut into 1-inch pieces

1 tomato, coarsely chopped, or 1 cup no-salt-added canned tomatoes, chopped with their juices

¾ cup pitted prunes, halved

19-ounce can chick-peas, rinsed and drained

⅓ cup chopped fresh parsley

1 cup couscous

2 cups boiling water

½ cup sliced almonds, toasted

1. In a medium saucepan, heat the oil until hot but not smoking over medium heat. Add the onion and garlic and cook, stirring frequently, until the onion is softened, about 7 minutes. Add the potatoes and cook, stirring frequently, until they begin to color, about 5 minutes. Stir in the cumin, paprika, ginger, and ½ teaspoon of the salt and cook, stirring, for 1 minute.

2. Add the carrots, tomato, prunes, and 2 cups of water to the pan and bring to a boil. Reduce to a simmer, cover, and cook until the potatoes are tender, about 10 minutes. Stir in the chick-peas and parsley and cook, stirring occasionally, until heated through, about 4 minutes.

3. Meanwhile, in a large bowl, combine the couscous, boiling water, and the remaining ¼ teaspoon salt. Stir well, cover, and let stand until the couscous has softened, about 5 minutes. Divide the couscous among 4 plates and spoon the stew alongside. Sprinkle the almonds over and serve.

Helpful hints: To toast the almonds, spread them out in a small baking pan and cook them in a 350° oven for 3 to 5 minutes; shake the pan occasionally to keep them from scorching, and turn them out of the pan as soon as they're crisp, fragrant, and lightly browned. You can use 1 cup raisins (dark or golden) instead of the prunes.

FAT: 13G/20%
CALORIES: 583
SATURATED FAT: 1.2G
CARBOHYDRATE: 103G
PROTEIN: 18G
CHOLESTEROL: 0MG
SODIUM: 602MG

French Bean and Mushroom Stew

Serves: 4
Working time: 30 minutes
Total time: 45 minutes

This peasant-style bean-and-vegetable stew is suffused with the tantalizing fragrances of dried mushrooms, rosemary, and sage.

1 ounce dried mushrooms, such as porcini (½ cup)

½ cup sun-dried (not oil-packed) tomato halves

2 cups boiling water

1 tablespoon olive oil

1 onion, finely chopped

2 leeks or 4 scallions, cut into ½-inch slices

4 cloves garlic, minced

2 carrots, halved lengthwise and thinly sliced

½ pound fresh mushrooms, thickly sliced

Two 19-ounce cans white kidney beans (cannellini), rinsed and drained

14½-ounce can no-salt-added stewed tomatoes, chopped with their juices

½ teaspoon salt

½ teaspoon dried rosemary

½ teaspoon dried sage

½ teaspoon freshly ground black pepper

1. In a medium bowl, combine the dried mushrooms, sun-dried tomatoes, and boiling water and let stand until softened, about 15 minutes. Scoop the dried mushrooms and tomatoes from their soaking liquid. Strain the liquid through a fine-mesh sieve or a paper towel-lined sieve and set aside. Coarsely chop the dried mushrooms and sun-dried tomatoes.

2. In a medium saucepan, heat the oil until hot but not smoking over medium-high heat. Add the onion, leeks, and garlic and cook, stirring frequently, until the onion and leeks are softened, about 7 minutes. Add the carrots and fresh mushrooms and cook, stirring frequently, until the carrots are tender, about 4 minutes.

3. Stir the beans, stewed tomatoes, salt, rosemary, sage, pepper, dried mushrooms, sun-dried tomatoes, and the reserved soaking liquid into the pan. Bring to a boil, reduce to a simmer, cover, and cook, stirring occasionally, until rich and flavorful, about 10 minutes. Divide the stew among 4 bowls and serve.

Helpful hint: The soaking liquid from the mushrooms and tomatoes is strained to remove any sand or grit that's been released by the dried mushrooms.

Fat: 6g/14%
Calories: 388
Saturated Fat: 0.6g
Carbohydrate: 68g
Protein: 21g
Cholesterol: 0mg
Sodium: 670mg

SKILLET DISHES

2

Wrapped in tender cornmeal crêpes, ratatouille (a Provençal vegetable stew) becomes an enticing main dish. Eggplant, bell peppers, zucchini, and tomatoes go into the ratatouille; we've added shredded mozzarella, too, for a more nourishing meal. Complement the crêpes with a colorful salad of red- and green-leaf lettuces and cherry tomatoes.

RATATOUILLE-FILLED CRÊPES

SERVES: 4
WORKING TIME: 40 MINUTES
TOTAL TIME: 45 MINUTES

½ cup yellow cornmeal

½ cup flour

1 teaspoon salt

1 egg white

¾ cup plus 1 tablespoon skimmed milk

2 teaspoons olive oil

3 cups peeled and cubed eggplant (½-inch cubes)

2 green bell peppers, coarsely diced

1 zucchini, cut into ½-inch cubes

2 tablespoons no-salt-added tomato paste

2 tablespoons red wine vinegar

1½ teaspoons dried basil

1 teaspoon dried oregano

1 cup canned no-salt-added tomatoes, chopped with their juices

2 teaspoons sugar

¼ teaspoon freshly ground black pepper

1½ cups shredded part-skim mozzarella cheese (6 ounces)

1. In a blender or food processor, combine the cornmeal, flour, ¼ teaspoon of the salt, the egg white, milk, and 1 teaspoon of the oil. Process to form a smooth batter. Spray a 6-inch nonstick skillet with nonstick cooking spray and preheat over medium heat. Spoon 2 tablespoons of the batter into the pan, tilting it so that the crêpe spreads to cover the bottom of the pan (see tip). Cook until lightly browned on one side and cooked through, about 30 seconds. Quickly turn the crêpe over and cook for 10 seconds. Transfer to a plate, cover with waxed paper, and repeat with the remaining batter, spraying the pan each time and separating the crêpes with waxed paper, for a total of 8 crêpes.

2. In a large nonstick skillet, heat the remaining 1 teaspoon oil until hot but not smoking over medium heat. Add the eggplant and bell peppers, cover, and cook, stirring occasionally, until the bell peppers are softened, about 6 minutes. Add the zucchini, tomato paste, vinegar, basil, and oregano; cover and cook until the zucchini is tender, about 6 minutes.

3. Stir the tomatoes, sugar, black pepper, and the remaining ¾ teaspoon salt into the pan. Divide the crêpes among 4 plates. Sprinkle each crêpe with 2 tablespoons of the mozzarella. Dividing evenly, top the cheese with the ratatouille. Sprinkle with the remaining mozzarella, roll up, and serve warm or at room temperature.

FAT: 10G/27%
CALORIES: 334
SATURATED FAT: 4.8G
CARBOHYDRATE: 44G
PROTEIN: 18G
CHOLESTEROL: 26MG
SODIUM: 807MG

TIP

After spooning the batter into the pan, tilt the pan to spread the batter into a thin, even round.

SERVES: 4
WORKING TIME: 30 MINUTES
TOTAL TIME: 30 MINUTES

There are three marvelous layers of texture and flavor in this unusual pasta dish. A bed of couscous—a pasta in the form of fine granules—cradles crisp-tender vegetables and black olives, which are in turn graced with a topping of feta, Parmesan, fresh basil, and toasted pine nuts. Greek Calamata olives make a tastier, more authentic dish than canned black olives.

¼ cup crumbled feta cheese

1 tablespoon grated Parmesan cheese

1 teaspoon olive oil

2 red bell peppers, cut into ¼-inch dice

1 onion, finely chopped

½ pound green beans, cut into ½-inch pieces

1 cup couscous

1¼ cups boiling water

¾ teaspoon salt

1 pound tomatoes, seeded and cut into ½-inch chunks

2 tablespoons chopped Calamata or other brine-cured black olives

1 teaspoon dried oregano

¼ teaspoon freshly ground black pepper

⅓ cup chopped fresh basil

2 tablespoons pine nuts, toasted

1. In a small bowl, combine the feta and Parmesan.

2. In a large nonstick skillet, heat the oil until hot but not smoking over medium heat. Add the bell peppers, onion, and green beans; cover and cook, stirring occasionally, until the green beans are crisp-tender, about 10 minutes.

3. Meanwhile, in a medium bowl, combine the couscous, boiling water, and ¼ teaspoon of the salt. Stir well, cover, and let stand until the couscous has softened, about 5 minutes.

4. Stir the tomatoes, olives, oregano, black pepper, and the remaining ½ teaspoon salt into the skillet and cook until the tomatoes are softened, about 3 minutes. Fluff the couscous with a fork and spread onto 4 plates. Spoon the vegetables over, top with the cheese mixture, sprinkle the basil and pine nuts over, and serve.

Helpful hint: To toast the pine nuts, place them in a small, dry skillet and cook over medium heat, stirring and shaking the pan, for 3 to 4 minutes, or until golden.

FAT: 8G/23%
CALORIES: 319
SATURATED FAT: 2.3G
CARBOHYDRATE: 54G
PROTEIN: 12G
CHOLESTEROL: 9MG
SODIUM: 626MG

Asian Vegetable Rolls

SERVES: 4
WORKING TIME: 30 MINUTES
TOTAL TIME: 30 MINUTES

2 tablespoons reduced-sodium soy sauce

2 tablespoons fresh lime juice

1 tablespoon minced fresh ginger

2½ teaspoons dark Oriental sesame oil

2 teaspoons honey

⅛ teaspoon ground cloves

1 whole egg

2 egg whites

¾ teaspoon sugar

1 red bell pepper, cut into thin slivers

1 cup shredded carrots

2 cups bean sprouts

1 cup canned black beans, rinsed and drained

3 scallions, slivered

8 large soft lettuce leaves, such as Boston or Bibb

1. In a small bowl, combine 4 teaspoons of the soy sauce, the lime juice, ginger, 1 teaspoon of the oil, the honey, and cloves.

2. In a small bowl, whisk together the whole egg, egg whites, sugar, and the remaining 2 teaspoons soy sauce. Spray an 8-inch nonstick skillet with nonstick cooking spray and preheat over medium-low heat. Add the egg mixture and cook until it is almost set on top, about 4 minutes. Flip the egg pancake over and cook until it is set, about 30 seconds. Transfer the pancake to a cutting board and when cool enough to handle, cut into thin strips.

3. In a large nonstick skillet, heat the remaining 1½ teaspoons oil until hot but not smoking over medium heat. Add the bell pepper and cook until softened, about 6 minutes. Stir in the carrots and bean sprouts and cook, stirring, for 1 minute. Stir in the egg strips, black beans, scallions, and 1 tablespoon of the soy-lime sauce. Cook until the beans are heated through, about 1 minute. Divide the lettuce leaves among 4 plates. Spoon the vegetables over and drizzle each with 1 teaspoon of the soy-lime sauce. Roll up the lettuce leaves, securing each with a toothpick. Serve the rolls with the remaining sauce on the side.

Helpful hint: You'll need 1 to 1½ heads of Boston or Bibb lettuce for 8 large leaves.

FAT: 5G/28%
CALORIES: 161
SATURATED FAT: 0.8G
CARBOHYDRATE: 22G
PROTEIN: 9G
CHOLESTEROL: 53MG
SODIUM: 491MG

The tender lettuce leaves in this Cantonese-style dish make a pleasant contrast to the warm stir-fried egg and vegetable mixture. Though ground beef is a more traditional filling, you'll find the protein-rich beans and crunchy vegetables deliciously satisfying. Lettuce leaves with a natural "cup" shape work well here; they're easy to wrap and then lift to your mouth without mishaps.

SKILLET RED BEANS AND RICE

SERVES: 4
WORKING TIME: 20 MINUTES
TOTAL TIME: 45 MINUTES

Red beans and rice, the pride of New Orleans, can be quite delicious (and is much healthier) without the usual ham or salt pork.

2 teaspoons olive oil

3 onions, finely chopped

2 carrots, halved lengthwise and thinly sliced

1¼ cups long-grain rice

1½ teaspoons dried thyme

1½ teaspoons dried oregano

14½-ounce can reduced-sodium vegetable broth

¾ cup dry white wine

1 cup frozen baby lima beans, thawed

1½ cups canned no-salt-added tomatoes, chopped with their juices

½ teaspoon salt

½ teaspoon freshly ground black pepper

15-ounce can red kidney beans, rinsed and drained

½ cup chopped fresh parsley

1 tablespoon fresh lime juice

1. In a large nonstick skillet, heat the oil until hot but not smoking over medium heat. Add the onions and carrots and cook until the onions are softened, about 5 minutes. Add the rice, thyme, and oregano and cook until fragrant, about 1 minute.

2. Stir the broth, wine, and 1 cup of water into the pan. Bring to a simmer, cover, and cook for 10 minutes. Stir in the lima beans, tomatoes, salt, and pepper and bring to a boil. Reduce to a simmer and cook until the rice is tender, about 8 minutes. Stir in the kidney beans and parsley, remove from the heat, cover, and let stand for 5 minutes to heat through. Stir in the lime juice and serve.

Helpful hint: Spice up the dish, if you like, with a few drops of hot pepper sauce—or just put the bottle on the table for those who like it.

FAT: 4G/7%
CALORIES: 488
SATURATED FAT: 0.5G
CARBOHYDRATE: 90G
PROTEIN: 17G
CHOLESTEROL: 0MG
SODIUM: 572MG

HUNAN STIR-FRY

SERVES: 4
WORKING TIME: 25 MINUTES
TOTAL TIME: 35 MINUTES

1 cup long-grain rice

¼ teaspoon salt

3 tablespoons reduced-sodium soy sauce

2 tablespoons rice vinegar

1 tablespoon molasses

1 tablespoon chili sauce

1 tablespoon minced fresh ginger

⅛ teaspoon cayenne pepper

¼ teaspoon hot pepper sauce

2 teaspoons cornstarch

2 teaspoons dark Oriental sesame oil

1½ cups peeled baby carrots

4 cups broccoli florets

1 green bell pepper, diced

1 yellow or red bell pepper, diced

4 scallions, cut on the diagonal into 1-inch pieces

2 cloves garlic, minced

⅓ cup finely chopped dry-roasted cashews

1. In a medium saucepan, bring 2¼ cups of water to a boil. Add the rice and salt, reduce to a simmer, cover, and cook until the rice is tender, about 17 minutes.

2. Meanwhile, in a small bowl, combine ¼ cup of water, the soy sauce, vinegar, molasses, chili sauce, ginger, cayenne, hot pepper sauce, and cornstarch, stirring to blend well.

3. In a large nonstick skillet or wok, heat the oil until hot but not smoking over medium-high heat. Add the carrots and broccoli and cook, stirring, until the carrots are crisp-tender, about 3 minutes. Add the bell peppers and stir-fry until the peppers are softened, about 4 minutes. Add the scallions, garlic, and cashews and cook, stirring, until fragrant, about 1 minute. Stir in the soy sauce mixture, bring to a boil, and cook, stirring, until slightly thickened, about 1 minute. Divide the rice among 4 plates, spoon the vegetable mixture alongside, and serve.

Helpful hint: The bold flavors of this dish would be especially effective with brown rice. If you choose to serve brown rice, be sure to allow for the longer cooking time (about 40 minutes total). Or, use quick-cooking brown rice, which is ready in 15 minutes.

FAT: 8G/20%
CALORIES: 361
SATURATED FAT: 1.4G
CARBOHYDRATE: 64G
PROTEIN: 11G
CHOLESTEROL: 0MG
SODIUM: 705MG

Spicy Hunan dishes often feature sweet and sour flavors. This one is packed with vegetables and served with rice.

ZUCCHINI AND GREEN PEA FRITTATA

SERVES: 4
WORKING TIME: 20 MINUTES
TOTAL TIME: 20 MINUTES

A frittata is an Italian dish consisting of beaten eggs and a filling—such as vegetables, leftover pasta, or cheese. Although it's similar to an omelete, a frittata is easier to prepare since the tricky step of folding the omelete over the other ingredients is eliminated. This frittata is filled with zucchini, peas, and herbs and is topped with Parmesan cheese.

2 whole eggs

5 egg whites

1 cup canned white kidney beans (cannellini), rinsed and drained

2 scallions, cut into 1-inch pieces

¾ teaspoon salt

¼ teaspoon hot pepper sauce

2 teaspoons olive oil

2 zucchini, quartered lengthwise and thinly sliced

2 tablespoons chopped fresh mint

½ teaspoon dried basil

1½ cups frozen peas

1 tablespoon balsamic vinegar

3 tablespoons grated Parmesan cheese

1. Preheat the broiler. In a blender or food processor, combine the whole eggs, egg whites, beans, scallions, salt, and hot pepper sauce and process until smooth.

2. In a medium broilerproof skillet, heat the oil until hot but not smoking over medium heat. Add the zucchini and cook until crisp-tender, about 5 minutes. Add the mint, basil, peas, and vinegar and cook until fragrant, about 1 minute.

3. Reduce the heat to low, add the egg mixture to the skillet, cover, and cook until the frittata is set around the edges but still liquid in the center, 6 to 8 minutes.

4. Place the skillet under the broiler 3 inches from the heat and cook for 2 to 5 minutes, or until golden brown and set in the center. Sprinkle the Parmesan over and broil for 1 minute, or until the cheese is golden. Cut into wedges, divide among 4 plates, and serve.

Helpful hint: If your skillet doesn't have a broilerproof handle, wrap the handle in a double layer of foil.

FAT: 7G/29%
CALORIES: 202
SATURATED FAT: 1.9G
CARBOHYDRATE: 19G
PROTEIN: 17G
CHOLESTEROL: 109MG
SODIUM: 741MG

Sizeable slices of zucchini, parsnip, and carrot, along with meaty chick-peas, are bathed in a lively sauce to make this hearty dinner dish. The accompanying couscous is steeped in carrot juice for a rich golden color and sweet, earthy flavor. A dollop of creamy yogurt supplies a cooling contrast to the spicy vegetables; cool drinks would be welcome, too.

CHUNKY VEGETABLE COUSCOUS

SERVES: 4
WORKING TIME: 35 MINUTES
TOTAL TIME: 40 MINUTES

2 teaspoons olive oil

2 carrots, cut into ½-inch slices

2 parsnips, peeled and cut into ½-inch slices

2 zucchini, halved lengthwise and sliced

1 teaspoon paprika

¾ teaspoon ground ginger

¾ teaspoon curry powder

¾ teaspoon dried thyme

¼ teaspoon cinnamon

¾ teaspoon salt

¼ teaspoon freshly ground black pepper

15-ounce can chick-peas, rinsed and drained

2 tablespoons firmly packed dark brown sugar

3 tablespoons fresh lemon juice

1 cup carrot juice (see tip)

1 cup couscous

½ cup plain low-fat yogurt

1. In a large nonstick skillet, heat the oil until hot but not smoking over medium heat. Add the carrots and parsnips. Cover and cook, stirring occasionally, until the carrots are crisp-tender, about 6 minutes. Add the zucchini, cover, and cook until the zucchini is softened, about 5 minutes.

2. Stir the paprika, ginger, curry powder, thyme, cinnamon, ½ teaspoon of the salt, and the pepper into the pan and cook until fragrant, about 2 minutes. Stir in the chick-peas, brown sugar, and 2 tablespoons of the lemon juice. Remove from the heat, cover, and let stand for 5 minutes to heat through.

3. Meanwhile, in a small saucepan, combine the carrot juice, ½ cup of water, the remaining ¼ teaspoon salt, and remaining 1 tablespoon lemon juice. Bring to a simmer, stir in the couscous, remove from the heat, cover, and let stand until the couscous has softened, about 5 minutes. Fluff the couscous with a fork and divide among 4 plates. Spoon the vegetable mixture alongside, top with a dollop of the yogurt, and serve.

Helpful hint: To save time when cooking, you can measure out and combine the spices, herbs, salt, and pepper used in step 2 well ahead of time.

FAT: 5G/11%
CALORIES: 412
SATURATED FAT: 0.8G
CARBOHYDRATE: 79G
PROTEIN: 14G
CHOLESTEROL: 2MG
SODIUM: 596MG

TIP

Carrot juice, which adds subtle sweetness and rich color, is an excellent source of beta carotene and potassium. You'll find it in health food stores, where it's made fresh, and in the refrigerated section of most supermarkets. You may also be able to find it canned, along with other fruit and vegetable juices, in your supermarket.

SAUTÉED VEGETABLES WITH PEANUT SAUCE

SERVES: 4
WORKING TIME: 35 MINUTES
TOTAL TIME: 35 MINUTES

Four 6-inch flour tortillas

1 tablespoon creamy peanut butter

1 tablespoon honey

1 tablespoon white wine vinegar

2 teaspoons minced fresh ginger

1 tablespoon plus 2 teaspoons Worcestershire sauce

¼ cup plus 1 tablespoon chopped fresh cilantro or basil

1 teaspoon vegetable oil

1 red bell pepper, cut into thin strips

1 green bell pepper, cut into thin strips

1 red onion, halved and thinly sliced

2 cloves garlic, minced

1 teaspoon dried thyme

1 teaspoon chili powder

1 cup frozen corn kernels

¾ cup diced firm, low-fat tofu

½ teaspoon salt

1. Preheat the oven to 350°. Wrap the tortillas in foil and place in the oven for 10 minutes, or until heated through. Meanwhile, in a small bowl, combine the peanut butter, honey, vinegar, ginger, 2 teaspoons of the Worcestershire sauce, 1 tablespoon of water, and 1 tablespoon of the cilantro.

2. In a large nonstick skillet, heat the oil until hot but not smoking over medium-high heat. Add the bell peppers, onion, garlic, thyme, and chili powder and cook until the peppers are softened, about 6 minutes. Stir in the corn, tofu, salt, and the remaining 1 tablespoon Worcestershire sauce. Cook until the corn and tofu are heated through, about 2 minutes.

3. Divide the tortillas among 4 plates. Spoon the vegetable mixture down the center of the tortillas, drizzle with the sauce, and garnish with the remaining ¼ cup cilantro. Fold the tortillas over or leave them open face and serve.

Helpful hint: Although most of the fat in tofu is unsaturated, it does derive more than 50 percent of its calories from fat. Newly available "light" tofu has 75 percent less fat than regular tofu. Look for light tofu in packages that keep without refrigeration (like long-life milk) so you can always have some on hand.

FAT: 6G/25%
CALORIES: 218
SATURATED FAT: 0.9G
CARBOHYDRATE: 36G
PROTEIN: 9G
CHOLESTEROL: 0MG
SODIUM: 512MG

From exotic Indonesia comes the idea of a peanuty salad dressing. While the traditional sauce is made with coconut milk, chilies, and peanut butter, our lighter version blends the peanut butter with honey and vinegar. The sauced vegetables are served in warm tortillas, making this a deliciously complete meal.

SWEET AND SOUR VEGETABLES

SERVES: 4
WORKING TIME: 25 MINUTES
TOTAL TIME: 30 MINUTES

*E*njoy *a colorful Chinese stir-fry without leaving home. Our recipe is considerably lower in fat than the restaurant version, too.*

1 cup long-grain rice

¾ teaspoon salt

1 tablespoon vegetable oil

½ pound mushrooms, halved

2 green bell peppers, cut into ½-inch-wide strips

1 red bell pepper, cut into ½-inch-wide strips

4 scallions, cut into 1-inch lengths

2 tablespoons grated fresh ginger

2 cloves garlic, minced

1 cup canned baby corn, cut into 1-inch lengths if large

1 cup cherry tomatoes

½ cup canned sliced water chestnuts

20-ounce can juice-packed pineapple chunks, drained, juice reserved

⅓ cup chili sauce

1½ teaspoons cornstarch

¼ cup chopped peanuts

1. In a medium saucepan, bring 2¼ cups of water to a boil. Add the rice and ¼ teaspoon salt, reduce to a simmer, cover, and cook until the rice is tender, about 17 minutes.

2. Meanwhile, in a large nonstick skillet, heat the oil until hot but not smoking over medium heat. Add the mushrooms and bell peppers and cook, stirring frequently, until the peppers are crisp-tender, about 5 minutes. Add the scallions, ginger, and garlic and cook until the scallions are softened, about 2 minutes.

3. Add the corn, tomatoes, water chestnuts, and pineapple chunks to the pan and cook until heated through, about 4 minutes. In a small bowl, combine the chili sauce, ½ cup of the reserved pineapple juice, the cornstarch, and the remaining ½ teaspoon salt. Stir into the vegetable mixture, bring to a boil, and cook, stirring constantly, until slightly thickened, about 1 minute. Divide the rice among 4 plates. Spoon the vegetable mixture over, sprinkle with the peanuts, and serve.

Helpful hint: If the fresh ginger you are using has thin skin, you don't need to peel it before grating. If the skin is thick and leathery, however, it's best to remove it with a vegetable peeler or paring knife.

FAT: 10G/21%
CALORIES: 440
SATURATED FAT: 1.2G
CARBOHYDRATE: 83G
PROTEIN: 11G
CHOLESTEROL: 0MG
SODIUM: 742MG

Skillet Spanish Rice

SERVES: 4
WORKING TIME: 20 MINUTES
TOTAL TIME: 40 MINUTES

2 teaspoons olive oil

1 leek, quartered lengthwise and thinly sliced, or 5 scallions, thinly sliced

2 zucchini, thinly sliced

1 red onion, halved and thinly sliced

1 teaspoon dried basil

1 teaspoon dried thyme

½ teaspoon turmeric

½ teaspoon salt

⅛ teaspoon freshly ground black pepper

1 cup long-grain rice

14½-ounce can reduced-sodium vegetable broth

¼ cup dry white wine

1 tablespoon cider vinegar

15-ounce can no-salt-added tomatoes, chopped and drained, juices reserved

1½ cups frozen peas

2 tablespoons grated Parmesan cheese

1. In a large nonstick skillet, heat the oil until hot but not smoking over medium-high heat. Add the leek, zucchini, and onion and cook until the onion begins to soften, about 4 minutes. Stir in the basil, thyme, turmeric, salt, and pepper and cook until fragrant, about 1 minute.

2. Add the rice to the pan, stirring to coat. Stir in the broth, wine, vinegar, reserved tomato liquid, and ½ cup of water and bring to a boil. Reduce to a simmer, cover, and cook for 15 minutes. Stir in the tomatoes and peas, cover, and cook until the rice is tender, about 5 minutes. Sprinkle the Parmesan over and serve.

Helpful hints: If you wish, omit the wine and substitute broth or water. You can substitute red or white wine vinegar for the cider vinegar, if you like.

FAT: 4G/11%
CALORIES: 340
SATURATED FAT: 1G
CARBOHYDRATE: 64G
PROTEIN: 11G
CHOLESTEROL: 2MG
SODIUM: 522MG

Onion, leek, zucchini, tomatoes, and peas turn this familiar side dish into a handsome green-and-gold entrée.

Try this rustic Italian dish as a change from run-of-the-mill sauced pastas. The diced fresh tomatoes form just one aspect of the complex sauce—fresh orange juice and zest, sage, and garlic are the counterparts. Subtleties also count in designing an appealing dish: Notice how the shape of the penne echoes that of the cut-up green beans and Parmesan shavings.

PASTA AND BEANS WITH TOMATO-ORANGE SAUCE

SERVES: 4
WORKING TIME: 20 MINUTES
TOTAL TIME: 30 MINUTES

¾ pound green beans, cut into 2-inch lengths

12 ounces penne pasta

1 tablespoon olive oil

4 cloves garlic, minced

1½ teaspoons dried sage

1½ pounds tomatoes, diced

1 tablespoon grated orange zest

¼ cup orange juice

1 tablespoon balsamic vinegar

¾ teaspoon salt

¼ teaspoon freshly ground black pepper

19-ounce can white kidney beans (cannellini), rinsed and drained

4 ounces Parmesan cheese, shaved (see tip)

1. In a large pot of boiling water, cook the green beans until crisp-tender, about 8 minutes. With a slotted spoon, transfer the beans to a bowl. Add the pasta to the boiling water and cook until tender. Drain well.

2. Meanwhile, in a large nonstick skillet, heat the oil until hot but not smoking over medium-low heat. Add the garlic and cook for 1 minute, until fragrant. Add the sage, tomatoes, orange zest, orange juice, vinegar, salt, and pepper. Increase the heat to high and cook, stirring, until heated through, about 2 minutes.

3. Add the green beans and the white beans to the skillet and cook until heated through, about 1 minute. Transfer the bean mixture to a large bowl and add the pasta and all but 1 ounce of the Parmesan. Top with the remaining Parmesan and serve.

Helpful hint: Instead of the Parmesan shavings, you can toss the pasta with 1 cup of grated Parmesan.

TIP

To make Parmesan shavings: Let a block of Parmesan come to room temperature. Use a vegetable peeler to scrape thin, ribbon-like shavings.

FAT: 14G/20%
CALORIES: 628
SATURATED FAT: 5.4G
CARBOHYDRATE: 97G
PROTEIN: 31G
CHOLESTEROL: 19MG
SODIUM: 923MG

Tex-Mex Soft Vegetable Tacos

SERVES: 4
WORKING TIME: 25 MINUTES
TOTAL TIME: 25 MINUTES

The filling for these generously stuffed tacos is a satisfying mixture of black beans, corn, mushrooms, zucchini, and onion in a spicy salsa sauce. There's Cheddar cheese and sour cream inside, too. Accompany the tacos with your favorite fixings, such as tomato wedges, chopped onion, and shredded lettuce— even some extra salsa, if you like.

Four 8-inch low-fat flour tortillas

1½ teaspoons olive oil

1 red onion, slivered

1 zucchini, quartered lengthwise and thinly sliced

1½ cups sliced mushrooms

2 teaspoons chili powder

1 teaspoon ground cumin

1½ cups frozen corn kernels

2 tablespoons no-salt-added tomato paste

¾ cup mild or medium-hot prepared salsa

15-ounce can black beans, rinsed and drained

3 tablespoons chopped fresh cilantro or parsley

¼ cup shredded Cheddar cheese

¼ cup reduced-fat sour cream

1. Preheat the oven to 350°. Wrap the tortillas in foil and place in the oven for 10 minutes, or until heated through.

2. Meanwhile, in a large nonstick skillet, heat the oil until hot but not smoking over medium-high heat. Add the onion, zucchini, and mushrooms and cook, stirring occasionally, until the onion is tender and the mushrooms have released their juices, about 8 minutes. Stir in the chili powder, cumin, and corn and cook until fragrant, about 2 minutes. Stir in the tomato paste, salsa, black beans, and cilantro and cook until heated through, about 2 minutes.

3. Divide the tortillas among 4 plates. Spoon the vegetables down the center of the tortillas, sprinkle with the Cheddar, and top with a dollop of sour cream. Roll up the tortillas, cut them in half if desired, and serve.

Helpful hint: For easy cleanup, spray the grater with nonstick cooking spray before shredding the cheese.

FAT: 9G/23%
CALORIES: 357
SATURATED FAT: 3G
CARBOHYDRATE: 59G
PROTEIN: 14G
CHOLESTEROL: 12MG
SODIUM: 717MG

INDIAN SPICED SWEET POTATOES AND CAULIFLOWER

SERVES: 4
WORKING TIME: 20 MINUTES
TOTAL TIME: 40 MINUTES

It's impossible to discuss Indian cuisine without including the infinite variety of meatless dishes. In a country with millions of vegetarians, meatless cooking is in its glory. Here, vegetables are simmered in a sweet-tart curry sauce. The curry powder is amplified with additional spices—ginger, fennel seeds, coriander, allspice, and pepper—for superb flavor.

1 cup basmati or long-grain rice
¾ teaspoon salt
2 teaspoons olive oil
2 onions, coarsely chopped
3 cloves garlic, minced
3 carrots, cut on the diagonal into ½-inch slices
1½ pounds sweet potatoes, peeled and cut into ½-inch cubes
14½-ounce can no-salt-added stewed tomatoes
1 teaspoon curry powder
1 teaspoon ground ginger
½ teaspoon fennel seeds, crushed
½ teaspoon ground coriander
¼ teaspoon ground allspice
⅛ teaspoon cayenne pepper
4 cups cauliflower florets
⅓ cup orange marmalade
1 tablespoon white wine vinegar
½ cup reduced-fat sour cream

1. In a medium saucepan, bring 2¼ cups of water to a boil. Add the rice and ¼ teaspoon of the salt, reduce to a simmer, cover, and cook until the rice is tender, about 17 minutes.

2. Meanwhile, in a large nonstick skillet, heat the oil until hot but not smoking over medium heat. Add the onions, garlic, and carrots and cook, stirring occasionally, until the onions begin to soften, about 4 minutes. Stir in the sweet potatoes, tomatoes, curry powder, ginger, fennel seeds, coriander, allspice, and cayenne. Reduce the heat to low, cover, and cook until the carrots and sweet potatoes are almost tender, about 12 minutes.

3. Add the cauliflower, marmalade, vinegar, and the remaining ½ teaspoon salt to the pan, stirring to combine. Cover and simmer until the cauliflower is tender, about 7 minutes. Divide the rice among 4 plates and spoon the vegetable mixture over. Top with a dollop of the sour cream and serve.

Helpful hint: Fennel seeds are usually sold whole. Crush them in a mortar and pestle or, if you don't have one, place the seeds in a plastic bag and crush them with a rolling pin.

FAT: 8G/14%
CALORIES: 533
SATURATED FAT: 2.5G
CARBOHYDRATE: 111G
PROTEIN: 14G
CHOLESTEROL: 10MG
SODIUM: 534MG

SOUTHWESTERN-STYLE SCRAMBLED EGGS

SERVES: 4
WORKING TIME: 25 MINUTES
TOTAL TIME: 40 MINUTES

There's just one egg yolk (and six nonfat egg whites) in these chili-cheese scrambled eggs. Serve warm flour or corn tortillas with the eggs.

1 cup nonfat cottage cheese

1 whole egg

6 egg whites

3 tablespoons plain dried bread crumbs

¼ teaspoon salt

¼ teaspoon hot pepper sauce

½ teaspoon olive oil

1 red bell pepper, finely diced

1 green bell pepper, finely diced

3 scallions, finely chopped

1 cup frozen corn kernels, thawed

1 teaspoon ground cumin

⅓ cup shredded jalapeño jack cheese

½ cup mild to medium prepared salsa

1. Place the cottage cheese in a fine-mesh sieve and let drain for about 15 minutes. In a blender or food processor, combine the drained cottage cheese, whole egg, egg whites, bread crumbs, salt, and hot pepper sauce and process until smooth.

2. In a large nonstick skillet, heat the oil until hot but not smoking over medium heat. Add the bell peppers and cook until softened, about 6 minutes. Add the scallions, corn, and cumin and cook until the bell peppers are tender, about 2 minutes.

3. Stir the egg mixture into the skillet and cook, stirring occasionally, until the eggs are set, 6 to 8 minutes. Divide the eggs among 4 plates, sprinkle the jack cheese over, top with the salsa, and serve.

Helpful hint: The jalapeño jack cheese makes this dish a bit spicy; you can substitute plain Monterey jack cheese if you prefer.

FAT: 6G/26%
CALORIES: 212
SATURATED FAT: 2.2G
CARBOHYDRATE: 22G
PROTEIN: 19G
CHOLESTEROL: 68MG
SODIUM: 832MG

CORN AND BEANS IN SALSA VERDE

SERVES: 4
WORKING TIME: 25 MINUTES
TOTAL TIME: 35 MINUTES

1 cup long-grain rice

¾ teaspoon salt

2 teaspoons olive oil

4 scallions, thinly sliced

2 cloves garlic, minced

1 green bell pepper, cut into ½-inch squares

1 pound tomatoes, diced

19-ounce can black beans, rinsed and drained

4½-ounce can chopped mild green chilies

¾ cup chopped fresh cilantro or basil

3 tablespoons fresh lime juice

½ teaspoon dried oregano

2 cups frozen corn kernels

¼ cup reduced-fat sour cream

½ cup shredded Monterey jack cheese (2 ounces)

1. In a medium saucepan, bring 2¼ cups of water to a boil. Add the rice and ¼ teaspoon of the salt, reduce to a simmer, cover, and cook until the rice is tender, about 17 minutes.

2. Meanwhile, in a large nonstick skillet, heat the oil until hot but not smoking over medium heat. Add 3 of the scallions and the garlic and cook, stirring frequently, until the scallions are tender, about 2 minutes. Add the bell pepper and cook, stirring frequently, until the pepper is crisp-tender, about 4 minutes.

3. Add the tomatoes, beans, chilies, cilantro, lime juice, oregano, and the remaining ½ teaspoon salt to the pan and bring to a boil. Reduce to a simmer, cover, and cook until slightly thickened, about 5 minutes. Stir in the corn and cook until heated through, about 5 minutes. Divide the rice among 4 plates. Spoon the vegetables alongside and top with a dollop of sour cream. Sprinkle the cheese and reserved scallion over and serve.

Helpful hint: Cilantro looks very much like flat-leaf parsley, but has a strong flavor that you'll recognize as one of the key elements of Tex-Mex cooking. If you don't find it at the supermarket, try an Asian or Mexican food store.

FAT: 11G/22%
CALORIES: 461
SATURATED FAT: 4.1G
CARBOHYDRATE: 79G
PROTEIN: 17G
CHOLESTEROL: 20MG
SODIUM: 927MG

The combination of beans, corn, and cheese adds up to lots of protein here. And there's plenty of Tex-Mex flavor, too.

63

Those ivory and orange noodles certainly make a festive dish, don't they? But wait—the orange pasta isn't pasta at all; it's actually wide strips of carrot that have been cooked along with the noodles. Cauliflower, spinach, tomatoes, and peas make this dish a very special pasta primavera; the creamy, low-fat sauce is a blend of tangy goat cheese and sour cream.

Vegetable "Pasta"

SERVES: 4
WORKING TIME: 35 MINUTES
TOTAL TIME: 35 MINUTES

4 carrots, peeled

10 ounces pappardelle pasta or wide "yolkless" egg noodles

4 ounces goat cheese

⅓ cup reduced-fat sour cream

2 tablespoons flour

2 teaspoons olive oil

4 scallions, thinly sliced

1½ cups cauliflower florets

2 cups coarsely chopped fresh spinach

1 cup frozen peas

1¼ teaspoons dried tarragon

2 cloves garlic, minced

2 cups cherry tomatoes, halved if large

½ teaspoon salt

1. Bring a large pot of water to a boil for the pasta. With a vegetable peeler, cut the carrots into long thin strips (see tip). Add the pasta to the water and cook until tender, adding the carrot strips for the last 1 minute of cooking. Reserving ¾ cup of the pasta cooking water, drain the pasta and carrots.

2. Meanwhile, in a small bowl, combine the goat cheese, sour cream, and flour, blending until smooth. In a large nonstick skillet, heat the oil until hot but not smoking over medium heat. Add the scallions, cauliflower, and spinach and cook, stirring occasionally, until the scallions and spinach are wilted, about 5 minutes.

3. Add the peas, tarragon, and garlic to the skillet and cook until heated through, about 2 minutes. Add the goat cheese mixture and reserved pasta cooking water, stirring until blended. Add the cherry tomatoes and salt and cook until slightly thickened and heated through, about 2 minutes. Divide the pasta and carrots among 4 plates, spoon the vegetable mixture over, and serve.

Helpful hint: Chèvre (French-style goat cheese) would be a good choice for this recipe, but you can use Greek feta cheese instead. Rinse the feta to remove some of the salty brine, then mash the cheese with a fork before blending it with the sour cream and flour.

FAT: 16G/28%
CALORIES: 520
SATURATED FAT: 7.9G
CARBOHYDRATE: 77G
PROTEIN: 23G
CHOLESTEROL: 29MG
SODIUM: 556MG

TIP

Use long, even strokes with a vegetable peeler to create noodle-like strips from the carrots. If you use large carrots, the "noodles" will be nice and wide.

SPICY VEGETABLE FRIED RICE

SERVES: 4
WORKING TIME: 25 MINUTES
TOTAL TIME: 40 MINUTES

1 cup basmati or long-grain rice

¼ teaspoon salt

1 tablespoon olive oil

1 red bell pepper, cut into thin strips

3 cups small broccoli florets

4 scallions, cut on the diagonal into ½-inch pieces

2 cloves garlic, minced

1 tablespoon grated fresh ginger

1 cup slivered snow peas

3 tablespoons reduced-sodium soy sauce

2 tablespoons chili sauce

1 tablespoon Worcestershire sauce

1 tablespoon white wine vinegar

½ teaspoon hot pepper sauce

4 ounces firm, low-fat tofu, cut into ½-inch cubes

1. In a medium saucepan, bring 2¼ cups of water to a boil. Add the rice and salt, reduce to a simmer, cover, and cook until the rice is tender, about 17 minutes.

2. In a large nonstick skillet, heat the oil until hot but not smoking over medium heat. Add the bell pepper and broccoli, cover, and cook, stirring occasionally, until the broccoli is crisp-tender, about 5 minutes. Add the scallions, garlic, and ginger and cook, stirring, until fragrant, about 2 minutes.

3. Add the snow peas, soy sauce, chili sauce, Worcestershire sauce, vinegar, hot pepper sauce, and cooked rice to the pan, stirring to coat evenly with the sauce. Add the tofu and cook, stirring, until heated through, about 2 minutes.

Helpful hint: Another fragrant long-grain rice, such as Texmati, can be substituted for the basmati rice, which is relatively expensive.

FAT: 5G/16%
CALORIES: 275
SATURATED FAT: 0.5G
CARBOHYDRATE: 52G
PROTEIN: 13G
CHOLESTEROL: 0MG
SODIUM: 829MG

Turning fried rice into a main dish is as easy as adding vegetables and tofu. This is an eggless fried rice (the tofu takes over as the protein source) laced with the flavors of fresh ginger and chilies. Unlike eggs and meat, tofu doesn't need to be cooked, so it's simply stirred into the rice until heated through and well coated with sauce.

CARIBBEAN SPICED VEGETABLES

SERVES: 4
WORKING TIME: 35 MINUTES
TOTAL TIME: 35 MINUTES

Bright as an island bouquet, this skillet meal is bursting with flavor. A blend of mango chutney, peanut butter, and lime juice forms a rich, tantalizing sauce for the brown-sugar-glazed sweet potatoes, peppers, summer squash, and onion. Steamed rice is the simple foil for the sauté.

1 cup long-grain rice

¾ teaspoon salt

1¼ pounds sweet potatoes, peeled and cut into ½-inch chunks

1 tablespoon olive oil

1 onion, cut into ½-inch chunks

5 cloves garlic, minced

3 bell peppers, mixed colors, cut into ½-inch squares

1 yellow summer squash, cut into ¼-inch dice

2 tablespoons firmly packed dark brown sugar

1 teaspoon ground ginger

1 cup reduced-sodium vegetable broth

¼ cup fresh lime juice

¼ cup mango chutney

2 tablespoons creamy peanut butter

1 teaspoon cornstarch

1. In a medium saucepan, bring 2¼ cups of water to a boil. Add the rice and ¼ teaspoon of the salt, reduce to a simmer, cover, and cook until the rice is tender, about 17 minutes. In a separate pot of boiling water, cook the sweet potatoes until tender, about 7 minutes. Drain.

2. Meanwhile, in a large nonstick skillet, heat the oil until hot but not smoking over medium heat. Add the onion and garlic and cook, stirring frequently, until the onion is crisp-tender, about 5 minutes. Add the bell peppers and squash, sprinkle with the brown sugar, ginger, and the remaining ½ teaspoon salt and cook until the peppers are crisp-tender, about 5 minutes. Add the sweet potatoes, stirring to coat.

3. In a small bowl, combine the broth, lime juice, chutney, peanut butter, and cornstarch. Pour over the vegetables, bring to a boil, and cook, stirring, until slightly thickened, about 1 minute. Serve with the rice.

Helpful hint: You can cook the sweet potatoes up to a day ahead of time and store them in the refrigerator until needed.

FAT: 8G/15%
CALORIES: 496
SATURATED FAT: 1.3G
CARBOHYDRATE: 97G
PROTEIN: 10G
CHOLESTEROL: 0MG
SODIUM: 712MG

VEGETARIAN SLOPPY JOES

SERVES: 4
WORKING TIME: 25 MINUTES
TOTAL TIME: 25 MINUTES

You won't miss the beef in these chili-bean sloppy joes. Serve steamed zucchini and carrot sticks with the hot, hearty sandwiches.

2 teaspoons olive oil

1 red onion, coarsely chopped

2 carrots, halved lengthwise and thinly sliced

1 zucchini, finely diced

1 teaspoon paprika

1 teaspoon dried basil

1 teaspoon chili powder

2 cloves garlic, minced

1 cup canned no-salt-added tomato purée

½ cup barbecue sauce

15-ounce can red kidney beans, rinsed and drained

1 tablespoon cider vinegar

4 hamburger rolls, split

1. In a large nonstick skillet, heat the oil until hot but not smoking over medium heat. Add the onion and carrots and cook until the onion is softened, about 5 minutes. Add the zucchini, paprika, basil, chili powder, and garlic and cook, stirring occasionally, until the carrots are crisp-tender, about 6 minutes.

2. Stir the tomato purée, barbecue sauce, beans, and vinegar into the pan. Reduce the heat to a simmer and cook until the mixture is slightly thickened and the vegetables are crisp-tender, about 5 minutes. Divide the hamburger rolls among 4 plates. Spoon the vegetable mixture onto the hamburger rolls and serve.

Helpful hint: Use a barbecue sauce with a smoky flavor for the "beefiest" taste.

FAT: 6G/17%
CALORIES: 313
SATURATED FAT: 1G
CARBOHYDRATE:54G
PROTEIN: 13G
CHOLESTEROL: 0MG
SODIUM: 665MG

BAKED & STUFFED

3

Vegetable Pot Pie

SERVES: 4
WORKING TIME: 20 MINUTES
TOTAL TIME: 50 MINUTES PLUS CHILLING TIME

Pot pies usually rely on chicken or turkey from a previous meal, but this vegetable version requires no leftovers. You can get a head start on the recipe, however, by preparing the pie crust the night before. The dough will be easier to handle, having been chilled overnight. Notice that low-fat Neufchâtel replaces half the usual shortening in the crust.

1¼ cups flour
1 tablespoon sugar
¼ teaspoon baking powder
¾ teaspoon salt
2 tablespoons reduced-fat cream cheese (Neufchâtel)
2 tablespoons solid vegetable shortening
⅓ cup nonfat plain yogurt
¾ pound small red potatoes, cut into ½-inch cubes
2½ cups low-fat (1%) milk
¼ teaspoon cayenne pepper
4 cups broccoli florets
1½ cups frozen pearl onions
1 cup frozen peas
1 cup frozen corn kernels
⅓ cup grated Parmesan cheese

1. In a medium bowl, stir together 1 cup of the flour, the sugar, baking powder, and ¼ teaspoon of the salt. With a pastry blender or two knives, cut in the cream cheese and vegetable shortening until the mixture resembles coarse meal. Stir in the yogurt until the dough just comes together. Flatten into a disk, wrap in plastic wrap, and refrigerate for at least 1 hour or overnight.

2. In a large pot of boiling water, cook the potatoes until tender, about 7 minutes. Drain.

3. Preheat the oven to 375°. In a large saucepan, whisk the milk into the remaining ¼ cup flour. Cook over medium heat, whisking constantly, until the sauce is slightly thickened and no floury taste remains, about 4 minutes. Whisk in the cayenne and remaining ½ teaspoon salt. Add the broccoli and pearl onions and cook, stirring frequently, until the broccoli is crisp-tender, about 5 minutes. Add the peas, corn, Parmesan, and potatoes, stirring to combine. Pour into a 9-inch deep-dish glass pie plate.

4. On a lightly floured surface, roll out the dough to a 13-inch round. Place over the vegetables, turn the overhang under, and flute with a fork. Make several slashes in the top of the dough to allow steam to escape. Place on a baking sheet and bake for 30 minutes, or until the crust is golden brown and the vegetables are piping hot. Cut into wedges and serve.

FAT: 13G/22%
CALORIES: 538
SATURATED FAT: 4.9G
CARBOHYDRATE: 86G
PROTEIN: 24G
CHOLESTEROL: 15MG
SODIUM: 779MG

This classic Tex-Mex breakfast dish—hearty enough to serve for supper—normally entails lots of frying: Fried eggs, placed atop refried beans, are covered with fried tomatoes, chilies, and onions. Our hearty low-fat interpretation is baked in the oven and has layers of sweet potatoes, spicy tomatoes, and mashed pinto beans; the eggs bake on top.

BAKED HUEVOS RANCHEROS

SERVES: 4
WORKING TIME: 20 MINUTES
TOTAL TIME: 35 MINUTES

2 pounds sweet potatoes, peeled
and thinly sliced

19-ounce can pinto beans, rinsed
and drained

3 scallions, thinly sliced

14½-ounce can no-salt-added
stewed tomatoes

¾ cup mild or medium-hot
prepared salsa

2 teaspoons olive oil

2 cloves garlic, minced

4 eggs

¼ teaspoon salt

Four 8-inch flour tortillas

¼ cup chopped fresh cilantro or
parsley

1. Preheat the oven to 400°. In a large pot of boiling water, cook the sweet potatoes until tender, about 7 minutes. Drain well and pat dry on paper towels.

2. Meanwhile, in a small bowl, mash the beans until not quite smooth. Stir in the scallions. In another small bowl, stir together the stewed tomatoes and salsa.

3. Place the oil and garlic in a 13 x 9-inch glass baking dish. Heat in the oven until hot but not smoking, about 5 minutes. Add the sweet potatoes, stirring to coat. Spoon the tomato mixture over the sweet potatoes. Spoon 4 mounds of the bean mixture over the tomato mixture, making a depression in each mound. Crack an egg into each depression (see tip), sprinkle with the salt, and bake for 15 minutes, or until the eggs are just set and the sauce is piping hot. Wrap the tortillas in foil and bake during the final 5 minutes of cooking time.

4. Divide the eggs, beans, and sweet potatoes among 4 plates; sprinkle with the cilantro and serve with the tortillas.

Helpful hint: To save time, you can halve the sweet potatoes and slice them in the food processor. Drop the halves through the feed tube, using the slicing blade.

TIP

With a spoon, make an egg-size hollow in the top of each mound of beans. Crack each egg and carefully drop into the depressions.

FAT: 11G/20%
CALORIES: 502
SATURATED FAT: 2.4G
CARBOHYDRATE: 83G
PROTEIN: 18G
CHOLESTEROL: 213MG
SODIUM: 835MG

This savory rice torte (called a *"timballo di riso"* in Italian) is a party-worthy main dish that makes entertaining easy because it can be baked a few hours ahead of time and allowed to cool to room temperature. The rice *"crust"* supports a cheese filling rich with sun-dried tomatoes and pine nuts and layered with spinach.

SPINACH, SUN-DRIED TOMATO, AND CHEESE TORTE

SERVES: 6
WORKING TIME: 30 MINUTES
TOTAL TIME: 1 HOUR 20 MINUTES PLUS COOLING TIME

1 cup long-grain rice

½ teaspoon salt

1 cup sun-dried (not oil-packed) tomatoes

2 cups boiling water

1 teaspoon olive oil

10-ounce package frozen chopped spinach, thawed

2 cups low-fat (1%) cottage cheese

1 cup part-skim ricotta cheese

2 tablespoons grated Parmesan cheese

2 whole eggs

3 egg whites

1 cup packed fresh basil leaves

2 tablespoons pine nuts

1. In a medium saucepan, bring 2¼ cups of water to a boil. Add the rice and ¼ teaspoon of the salt, reduce to a simmer, cover, and cook until the rice is tender, about 17 minutes. Cool to room temperature. Meanwhile, in a small bowl, combine the sun-dried tomatoes and boiling water and let stand for 15 minutes, until softened. Drain and coarsely chop the tomatoes.

2. Preheat the oven to 375°. Spray a 9-inch springform pan with nonstick cooking spray. Spoon the rice into the bottom of the pan and cover with plastic wrap or waxed paper (see tip; top photo). Use a measuring cup to press the rice into an even layer on the bottom of the pan and to make it come up about a ½ inch on the sides (middle and bottom photos). Set aside. In a small bowl, combine the oil and spinach.

3. In a food processor, combine the cottage cheese, ricotta, Parmesan, whole eggs, egg whites, basil, and the remaining ¼ teaspoon salt. Process until smooth. Add the sun-dried tomatoes and pine nuts and process just to combine. Pour half of the cheese mixture over the rice in the prepared pan. Top with a layer of the spinach mixture, and pour the remaining cheese mixture on top. Place on a baking sheet and bake for 50 to 60 minutes, or until just set. Cool to room temperature, cut into 6 wedges, and serve.

FAT: 9G/24%
CALORIES: 338
SATURATED FAT: 3.7G
CARBOHYDRATE: 40G
PROTEIN: 25G
CHOLESTEROL: 88MG
SODIUM: 667MG

T I P

BAKED MANICOTTI

SERVES: 4
WORKING TIME: 35 MINUTES
TOTAL TIME: 55 MINUTES

8 manicotti shells (5 ounces)

19-ounce can chick-peas, rinsed and drained

1½ cups jarred roasted red peppers, rinsed and drained

3 cloves garlic, peeled

3 tablespoons plain dried bread crumbs

2 tablespoons whole unblanched almonds

1 tablespoon no-salt-added tomato paste

1½ teaspoons ground cumin

¾ teaspoon dried oregano

½ teaspoon salt

¼ teaspoon cayenne pepper

14½-ounce can no-salt-added stewed tomatoes

8-ounce can no-salt-added tomato sauce

¾ teaspoon ground coriander

1 cup shredded part-skim mozzarella cheese (4 ounces)

1 tablespoon chopped fresh parsley (optional)

1. In a large pot of boiling water, cook the manicotti until just tender. Drain well.

2. Preheat the oven to 425°. In a food processor, combine the chick-peas, roasted peppers, garlic, bread crumbs, almonds, tomato paste, cumin, oregano, salt, and cayenne and process until almost smooth but with some texture.

3. In an 11 x 7-inch glass baking dish, combine the stewed tomatoes, the tomato sauce, and coriander. Spoon the chick-pea mixture into a pastry bag with no tip attached. Pipe the chick-pea mixture into the cooked manicotti shells. Transfer the filled shells to the baking dish and spoon some of the sauce over. Cover with foil and bake for 20 minutes, or until the manicotti are piping hot and the sauce is bubbly. Uncover, sprinkle the mozzarella over, and bake for about 4 minutes, or until the cheese is melted. Divide among 4 plates, sprinkle the parsley over, and serve.

Helpful hint: Instead of using a pastry bag, you can fill a sturdy plastic bag with the filling, snip off one of the bottom corners, and pipe the filling into the manicotti shells.

FAT: 10G/22%
CALORIES: 415
SATURATED FAT: 3.3G
CARBOHYDRATE: 62G
PROTEIN: 20G
CHOLESTEROL: 16MG
SODIUM: 744MG

Instead of a fat-laden filling of meat or cheese (or both), these pasta tubes are stuffed with a robust mixture of chick-peas, roasted peppers, bread crumbs, almonds, and tomato paste. The manicotti are baked atop coriander-scented tomato sauce and crowned with part-skim mozzarella. Serve the pasta with sautéed zucchini and red onions, and a lettuce-and-radish salad.

CHILI-CREAM ENCHILADAS

SERVES: 4
WORKING TIME: 25 MINUTES
TOTAL TIME: 40 MINUTES

This Mexican favorite—stuffed with a rich cheese mixture—is sure to please. The "cream" sauce is made with low-fat milk.

2 cups low-fat (1%) cottage cheese

1 cup shredded Cheddar cheese (4 ounces)

3 tablespoons mango chutney

2 teaspoons Dijon mustard

Eight 6-inch corn tortillas

2½ cups low-fat (1%) milk

3 tablespoons flour

2 jalapeño peppers, seeded and finely chopped

1½ teaspoons chili powder

⅛ teaspoon cayenne pepper

1 cup frozen corn kernels

1 tablespoon chopped fresh parsley (optional)

1. Preheat the oven to 400°. In a medium bowl, combine the cottage cheese, ¾ cup of the Cheddar, the chutney, and mustard. Spread the mixture evenly over the tortillas. Roll up the tortillas and place in an 11 x 7-inch glass baking dish.

2. In a medium saucepan, whisk the milk into the flour. Stir in the jalapeños, chili powder, and cayenne and cook over medium heat, whisking constantly, until slightly thickened, about 4 minutes. Stir in the corn and spoon over the filled tortillas.

3. Cover the enchiladas with foil and bake for about 15 minutes, or until the sauce is piping hot and bubbly. Sprinkle with the remaining ¼ cup Cheddar and the parsley and serve.

Helpful hints: Fresh jalapeños and similar hot peppers contain volatile oils that can burn the skin—when working with them, wear plastic gloves. For a milder dish, you can use one 4½-ounce can chopped mild green chilies, drained, instead of the jalapeños.

FAT: 14G/27%
CALORIES: 474
SATURATED FAT: 7.9G
CARBOHYDRATE: 57G
PROTEIN: 31G
CHOLESTEROL: 40MG
SODIUM: 995MG

MEXICAN-STYLE STUFFED ZUCCHINI

SERVES: 4
WORKING TIME: 15 MINUTES
TOTAL TIME: 55 MINUTES

4 zucchini (8 ounces each), halved lengthwise

½ cup long-grain rice

4 scallions, thinly sliced

¼ teaspoon salt

1½ cups canned black beans, rinsed and drained

⅔ cup mild or medium-hot prepared salsa

1 cup canned no-salt-added tomato sauce

¼ cup chopped fresh cilantro or parsley

1 cup shredded jalapeño jack cheese (4 ounces)

1. With a paring knife, cut the flesh from the zucchini, leaving a ¼-inch-thick shell. Discard the zucchini flesh.

2. In a medium saucepan, bring 1⅓ cups of water to a boil. Add the rice, scallions, and salt. Reduce to a simmer, cover, and cook until the rice is tender, about 17 minutes. Transfer to a bowl and stir in the beans and ⅓ cup of the salsa.

3. Preheat the oven to 400°. Cut a small slice from the bottom side of each zucchini shell so that it will sit flat. In an 11 x 7-inch glass baking dish, combine the remaining ⅓ cup of salsa, the tomato sauce, and cilantro. Place the zucchini shells on top of the sauce, spoon the rice mixture into the shells, cover with foil, and bake for about 20 minutes, or until the filling is piping hot and the zucchini shells are tender.

4. Uncover the dish, sprinkle the cheese over, and bake for about 1 minute or until the cheese is melted. Spoon the sauce over the stuffed zucchini before serving.

Helpful hint: Jalapeño jack is Monterey jack cheese flecked with bits of jalapeño. If you can't get it, use Monterey jack or sharp Cheddar.

FAT: 10G/28%
CALORIES: 320
SATURATED FAT: 5.1G
CARBOHYDRATE: 43G
PROTEIN: 16G
CHOLESTEROL: 30MG
SODIUM: 728MG

T hese rice-stuffed zucchini boats "float" in a tomato sauce spiked with salsa and cilantro.

81

COUSCOUS-STUFFED PEPPER HALVES

SERVES: 4
WORKING TIME: 20 MINUTES
TOTAL TIME: 45 MINUTES

It's a particular pleasure to serve these stuffed peppers because the filling is so easy to prepare. Instead of rice, red and green bell peppers are filled with couscous, a tiny pasta that requires just 5 minutes of steeping. Raisins, shredded carrots, and cubes of mozzarella are mixed into the couscous. Tender leaf lettuce tossed with sweet red onions would go well with this dish.

2 red bell peppers, stemmed and halved lengthwise

2 green bell peppers, stemmed and halved lengthwise

4 cloves garlic, minced

2 carrots, shredded

¾ teaspoon salt

½ teaspoon ground ginger

1½ cups couscous

⅓ cup raisins

6 ounces part-skim mozzarella cheese, cut into ½-inch cubes

14½-ounce can no-salt-added stewed tomatoes, chopped with their juices

8-ounce can no-salt-added tomato sauce

¼ cup chopped fresh mint or basil

1. In a large pot of boiling water, cook the bell peppers for 3 minutes to blanch. Drain.

2. Preheat the oven to 375°. In a medium saucepan, bring 3 cups of water to a boil. Add the garlic, carrots, salt, and ginger and boil for 1 minute. Add the couscous, remove from the heat, cover, and let stand until tender, about 5 minutes. Stir in the raisins and mozzarella and set aside.

3. In a 13 x 9-inch glass baking dish, combine the stewed tomatoes, tomato sauce, and mint. Add the bell peppers, cut-sides up, and spoon in the couscous filling. Cover with foil and bake for about 20 minutes, or until the peppers are tender and the sauce is piping hot. Divide the pepper halves among 4 plates, spoon the tomato sauce over, and serve.

Helpful hint: To prepare the bell peppers for stuffing, use a paring knife to cut around the stem of each pepper. Gently remove the stems and cut the peppers in half. Discard the seeds and ribs.

FAT: 8G/14%
CALORIES: 506
SATURATED FAT: 4.4G
CARBOHYDRATE: 88G
PROTEIN: 23G
CHOLESTEROL: 25MG
SODIUM: 669MG

Bulghur (pre-steamed cracked wheat), combined with vegetables, mushrooms, pecans, and dill, takes the place of ground beef in this light adaptation of an old-fashioned recipe. If the cabbage leaves you are using are thick and hard to fold, use a sharp knife to cut away some of the outer rib of each leaf.

STUFFED CABBAGE WITH DILL SAUCE

SERVES: 4
WORKING TIME: 25 MINUTES
TOTAL TIME: 1 HOUR

1 small head cabbage (1 pound), cored

1 teaspoon olive oil

6 scallions, thinly sliced

2 carrots, quartered lengthwise and thinly sliced

1 zucchini, halved lengthwise and thinly sliced

¼ pound mushrooms, coarsely chopped

1 cup bulghur (cracked wheat)

2 tablespoons boiling water

½ teaspoon grated lemon zest

1 tablespoon fresh lemon juice

¾ cup snipped fresh dill

½ teaspoon salt

2 tablespoons chopped pecans (¾ ounce)

2 cups reduced-sodium vegetable broth

1¼ teaspoons cornstarch mixed with 1 tablespoon water

3 tablespoons reduced-fat sour cream

1. Preheat the oven to 400°. In a large pot of boiling water, cook the whole head of cabbage until it is crisp-tender and the leaves are easily separated, about 5 minutes. Drain. When cool enough to handle, separate into leaves, selecting the 12 largest leaves for stuffing. (Save the remainder for another use.)

2. In a medium saucepan, heat the oil until hot but not smoking over medium heat. Add the scallions and cook until softened, about 1 minute. Add the carrots, zucchini, and mushrooms and cook, stirring frequently, until the carrots are softened, about 4 minutes. Add the bulghur, boiling water, lemon zest, lemon juice, ½ cup of the dill, and the salt. Let stand until the bulghur is slightly chewy, about 10 minutes. Remove from the heat and stir in the pecans.

3. Using a ½-cup measuring cup as a mold, stuff the 12 cabbage leaves with the bulghur mixture and place them, seam-side down, in a 13 x 9-inch baking dish (see tip). Pour the broth over, cover with foil, and bake for about 25 minutes, or until the leaves are tender and the filling is heated through. Transfer the cabbage packets to 4 plates. Transfer the broth from the baking dish to a small saucepan and bring to a boil. Add the cornstarch mixture and cook, stirring constantly, until slightly thickened, about 1 minute. Stir in the remaining ¼ cup dill. Spoon the sauce over the cabbage packets, top with a dollop of sour cream, and serve.

FAT: 7G/24%
CALORIES: 266
SATURATED FAT: 1.3G
CARBOHYDRATE: 46G
PROTEIN: 10G
CHOLESTEROL: 4MG
SODIUM: 454MG

TIP

Fit a cabbage leaf into a ½-cup measuring cup, then spoon in the filling and fold the leaf over it to form a round packet. Invert the cup to place the cabbage packet in the baking pan.

Three-Pepper Pizza

Serves: 4
Working time: 10 minutes
Total time: 45 minutes

4 bell peppers, mixed colors

1 tablespoon yellow cornmeal

1 cup chopped fresh basil

2 tablespoons grated Parmesan cheese

1 pound store-bought pizza dough

1 red onion, cut into thin rings

2 tomatoes, thickly sliced

1 cup shredded part-skim mozzarella cheese (4 ounces)

1. Preheat the broiler. Cut off the four sides of each bell pepper and remove the ribs. Broil the peppers, cut-sides down, for about 10 minutes, or until the skin is charred. When cool enough to handle, peel and cut into ½-inch-wide strips. Turn the oven to 450°.

2. Lightly dust a baking sheet with the cornmeal. Knead ½ cup of the basil and the Parmesan into the pizza dough and flatten the pizza dough into a round. Place the dough on the cornmeal and press out to a 10-inch round. Cover the dough with the onion and tomatoes and bake on the bottom shelf of the oven for about 20 minutes, or until the crust is lightly browned.

3. Sprinkle with the mozzarella and the remaining ½ cup basil, top with the pepper slices, and bake for about 5 minutes, or until the cheese has melted and the peppers are piping hot.

Helpful hints: You can buy ready-to-use pizza dough from many pizzerias and Italian specialty stores; you may also find it in the dairy case in the supermarket. Or, you can use the refrigerated dough that comes in a roll. Either type of dough can be patted out into a rectangle, rather than rolled into a circle, if you like.

Roasted peppers, a popular pizza topping, make for a striking pie when a mix of red, yellow, and green bell peppers is used. Char the peppers thoroughly under the broiler. That way they'll not only be easier to peel, but they'll also have a more intensely smoky flavor. This pizza is a snap to fix because we use prepared pizza dough.

Fat: 10g/20%
Calories: 444
Saturated Fat: 4.2g
Carbohydrate: 70g
Protein: 20g
Cholesterol: 18mg
Sodium: 817mg

Halved, hollowed eggplants make attractive edible bowls. A traditional recipe for this favorite Italian dish fills the eggplant shells with sausage, but we take a lighter route: The diced eggplant cut from the shells is sautéed and mixed with tomatoes, pinto beans, part-skim ricotta and cottage cheese, and cubes of bread.

EGGPLANT STUFFED WITH RICOTTA CHEESE

SERVES: 4
WORKING TIME: 20 MINUTES
TOTAL TIME: 45 MINUTES PLUS COOLING TIME

2 eggplants (1 pound each)

2 teaspoons olive oil

6 scallions, thinly sliced

3 cloves garlic, minced

1½ cups chopped canned no-salt-added tomatoes

15-ounce can pinto beans, rinsed and drained

½ cup chopped fresh basil

½ teaspoon salt

¼ teaspoon freshly ground black pepper

½ cup low-fat (1%) cottage cheese

½ cup part-skim ricotta cheese

1 cup unseasoned stuffing mix

1 tablespoon slivered almonds

1. Preheat the oven to 400°. Halve the eggplants lengthwise. With a paring knife, cut the pulp from the eggplants, leaving a ½-inch-thick shell (see tip; top photo). Cut the removed pulp into ½-inch chunks (bottom photo). Transfer the shells to a 13 x 9-inch glass baking dish.

2. In a large nonstick skillet, heat the oil until hot but not smoking over medium heat. Add the scallions and garlic and cook, stirring frequently, until the scallions are softened, about 1 minute. Add the diced eggplant, stirring to coat. Stir in the tomatoes, beans, basil, salt, and pepper and bring to a boil. Reduce to a simmer and cook until slightly thickened, about 5 minutes. Transfer the eggplant mixture to a bowl and cool to room temperature.

3. Stir the cottage cheese, ricotta, stuffing mix, and almonds into the eggplant mixture. Spoon the mixture into the eggplant shells and bake for about 25 minutes, or until the filling is piping hot and the shells are tender. Divide among 4 plates and serve.

Helpful hint: Unseasoned stuffing mix is simply cubes of dried bread. If you have some stale white, Italian, or French bread on hand, you can cut it into cubes and use it instead. If the bread is not completely dry, spread the cubes on a baking sheet and bake them in a 350° oven for about 10 minutes.

FAT: 8G/23%
CALORIES: 317
SATURATED FAT: 2.4G
CARBOHYDRATE: 47G
PROTEIN: 18G
CHOLESTEROL: 11MG
SODIUM: 775MG

TIP

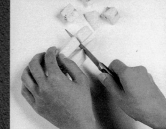

Use a sharp paring knife to cut the pulp from the eggplant halves, leaving a ½-inch shell. Cut the pulp into strips, then cut the strips crosswise into chunks.

Baked Polenta Cakes

SERVES: 4
WORKING TIME: 20 MINUTES
TOTAL TIME: 55 MINUTES

Polenta is the Italian word for an exceedingly common American ingredient—cornmeal. The Italian idea is to cook the meal into a very thick "mush" and treat it to savory seasonings that often include sharp cheese. Here molded, baked polenta cakes contain corn kernels and bits of roasted pepper as well as two kinds of cheese: jalapeño jack and Parmesan. Garnish the cakes with greens.

3 cups low-fat (1%) milk
1 cup plus 2 tablespoons yellow cornmeal
¾ cup shredded jalapeño jack cheese (3 ounces)
2 tablespoons grated Parmesan cheese
2 tablespoons reduced-fat sour cream
1 cup frozen corn kernels
⅔ cup jarred roasted red peppers, coarsely chopped
½ teaspoon salt

1. Preheat the oven to 450°. In a medium bowl, combine 1½ cups of the milk and the cornmeal. In a large heavy-bottomed saucepan, heat the remaining 1½ cups milk over medium heat until just simmering. Add the cornmeal mixture and cook, stirring constantly, until the mixture leaves the sides of the saucepan and is very thick, about 10 minutes. Remove from the heat and stir in the jalapeño jack, Parmesan, and sour cream. Stir in the corn, roasted peppers, and salt.

2. Spray four 1¼-cup soufflé dishes with nonstick cooking spray and pack the polenta mixture into the dishes. Bake for about 25 minutes, or until golden brown and firm. Set aside to cool for 10 minutes, then invert the polenta cakes onto 4 plates and serve.

Helpful hint: You can cook the polenta mixture in a 5-cup soufflé dish and cut it into wedges to serve instead of making individual portions. The baking time will be the same.

FAT: 12G/29%
CALORIES: 376
SATURATED FAT: 6G
CARBOHYDRATE: 50G
PROTEIN: 17G
CHOLESTEROL: 34MG
SODIUM: 609MG

BAKED VEGETABLE, RICE, AND NOODLE PILAF

SERVES: 4
WORKING TIME: 25 MINUTES
TOTAL TIME: 45 MINUTES

Don't choose between rice and pasta: Have both! Vegetables, mushrooms, almonds, and Cheddar round out this filling main dish.

2 teaspoons olive oil

1 onion, finely chopped

1 green bell pepper, cut into ½-inch squares

½ pound mushrooms, thinly sliced

3 ounces vermicelli noodles, broken into 2-inch lengths

1 cup long-grain rice

2½ cups reduced-sodium vegetable broth

⅓ cup snipped fresh dill

½ teaspoon salt

1 cup frozen peas

2 tablespoons sliced almonds

¾ cup shredded Cheddar cheese (3 ounces)

1. Preheat the oven to 350°. In a nonstick Dutch oven or flame-proof casserole, heat the oil until hot but not smoking over medium heat. Add the onion and cook, stirring frequently, until softened, about 7 minutes. Add the bell pepper and mushrooms and cook, stirring frequently, until the pepper is crisp-tender, about 4 minutes.

2. Increase the heat to high, add the vermicelli and rice, stirring until coated. Add the broth, dill, salt, and 1 cup of water and bring to a boil. Cover and transfer to the oven. Bake for about 17 minutes, or until the rice and noodles are tender. Stir in the peas, almonds, and Cheddar; cover, return to the oven, and bake for about 5 minutes, or until the cheese is melted and the peas are heated through.

Helpful hint: Vermicelli are fine pasta strands. They are often sold folded into "nests" rather than straight, like spaghetti. You may find them labeled with their Spanish name, "fideos."

FAT: 12G/24%
CALORIES: 456
SATURATED FAT: 5.1G
CARBOHYDRATE: 70G
PROTEIN: 17G
CHOLESTEROL: 22MG
SODIUM: 613MG

Mediterranean Baked Pasta

SERVES: 4
WORKING TIME: 20 MINUTES
TOTAL TIME: 50 MINUTES

12 ounces lasagna noodles, broken into fourths

1¾ cups low-fat (1%) cottage cheese

⅔ cup part-skim ricotta cheese

⅔ cup evaporated low-fat or skimmed milk

1 cup canned no-salt-added tomatoes, chopped with their juices

3 tablespoons no-salt-added tomato paste

1 whole egg, lightly beaten

2 egg whites, lightly beaten

2 tablespoons grated Parmesan cheese

1 teaspoon ground cinnamon

½ teaspoon salt

½ teaspoon freshly ground black pepper

1 cup frozen Italian flat green beans

⅓ cup chopped fresh mint

1. Preheat the oven to 350°. Spray an 11 x 7-inch ceramic or glass baking dish with nonstick cooking spray. In a large pot of boiling water, cook the lasagna noodles until tender. Drain well.

2. Meanwhile, in a food processor, combine the cottage cheese, ricotta, and evaporated milk and process until smooth and creamy, about 1 minute. Transfer to a large bowl and stir in the tomatoes, tomato paste, whole egg, egg whites, Parmesan, cinnamon, salt, and pepper. Fold in the green beans and mint. Add the cooked pasta and transfer the mixture to the prepared baking dish. Bake for about 30 minutes, or until set and slightly crisped.

Helpful hint: If fresh mint is not available, try ½ teaspoon dried oregano (another favorite Greek herb) as a substitute.

FAT: 9G/15%
CALORIES: 560
SATURATED FAT: 3.7G
CARBOHYDRATE: 82G
PROTEIN: 37G
CHOLESTEROL: 79MG
SODIUM: 878MG

Greek pastitsio is the inspiration here, but our creamy sauce is far lighter than the original.

Don't believe your eyes: That's not a beefburger you're looking at, it's a bean cake. Veggie burgers used to be high-fat items made from nuts and cheese, but our updated rendition is based on black beans, which are an excellent low-fat protein source. Nothing as ordinary as ketchup will do for these patties—they're sauced with a citrus "salsa."

Black Bean Cakes with Orange Relish

SERVES: 4
WORKING TIME: 20 MINUTES
TOTAL TIME: 40 MINUTES

6 cloves garlic, peeled

Two 19-ounce cans black beans, rinsed and drained

¼ cup plain dried bread crumbs

6 scallions, thinly sliced

1 tablespoon chili powder

¾ teaspoon ground cumin

½ teaspoon freshly ground black pepper

½ teaspoon salt

2 navel oranges

1 tomato, cut into ¼-inch dice

½ cup diced avocado

¼ cup chopped fresh parsley

2 tablespoons chili sauce

2 tablespoons fresh lime juice

1. Preheat the oven to 400°. In a small pot of boiling water, cook the garlic until softened, about 4 minutes. Transfer to a medium bowl and mash with a potato masher or fork. Add the beans and mash until not quite smooth, with some texture. Stir in the bread crumbs, scallions, 2½ teaspoons of the chili powder, the cumin, pepper, and salt.

2. Spray a baking sheet with nonstick cooking spray. With a cup measure, spoon four mounds of the bean mixture onto the baking sheet, spacing them 2 inches apart. Flatten the mounds to form four 6-inch round patties. Bake until the patties are heated through and slightly crisp on the outside, about 20 minutes.

3. Meanwhile, peel the oranges and, working over a small bowl to catch any juices, cut into sections (see tip). Cut the sections into ½-inch chunks and transfer to a large bowl. Add the tomato, avocado, parsley, chili sauce, lime juice, the remaining ½ teaspoon chili powder, and 2 tablespoons of the reserved orange juice. With a spatula, transfer the patties to 4 plates. Spoon the orange relish over and serve.

Helpful hint: The relish can be made up to 4 hours ahead of time. The acid in the citrus juices will keep the avocado from darkening. Refrigerate the relish in a covered container until needed.

FAT: 5G/16%
CALORIES: 282
SATURATED FAT: 0.7G
CARBOHYDRATE: 48G
PROTEIN: 14G
CHOLESTEROL: 0MG
SODIUM: 912MG

TIP

To prepare the oranges, remove the peel and, using a small knife, trim away all the bitter white pith. Working over a sieve set over a bowl to catch the juices, cut between the membranes to release the orange sections.

BAKED EGGPLANT ROLL-UPS

SERVES: 4
WORKING TIME: 25 MINUTES
TOTAL TIME: 50 MINUTES

2 eggplants (1 pound each)

1 cup low-fat (1%) cottage cheese

¼ cup part-skim ricotta cheese

⅓ cup plus 2 tablespoons grated Parmesan cheese

3 scallions, thinly sliced

½ cup chopped fresh mint

½ teaspoon salt

1 egg, lightly beaten

10-ounce package frozen chopped spinach, thawed and squeezed dry

½ cup plain dried bread crumbs

14½-ounce can no-salt-added stewed tomatoes, chopped with their juices

8-ounce can no-salt-added tomato sauce

1 tablespoon no-salt-added tomato paste

1. Preheat the oven to 400°. Cut a thin slice off both sides of each eggplant to remove some of the skin. Slice off the stems and bottom ends. Slice each eggplant lengthwise into 6 slices. In a large pot of boiling water, cook the eggplant slices for 1½ minutes to soften. Drain and pat dry on paper towels.

2. In a medium bowl, combine the cottage cheese, ricotta, ⅓ cup of the Parmesan, the scallions, ¼ cup of the mint, ¼ teaspoon of the salt, and the egg. Add the spinach and stir until well combined. Sprinkle one side of the eggplant slices evenly with the bread crumbs. Spoon the cheese-spinach mixture over the bread crumbs and roll each eggplant slice up.

3. In a 13 x 9-inch glass baking dish, combine the tomatoes, tomato sauce, tomato paste, the remaining ¼ cup mint, and remaining ¼ teaspoon salt. Place the eggplant rolls, seam-sides down, in the pan, cover with foil, and bake for about 25 minutes, or until piping hot. Uncover, sprinkle with the remaining 2 tablespoons Parmesan, and bake for 1 minute, or until the cheese has melted. Divide the eggplant rolls among 4 plates, spoon the sauce over, and serve.

Helpful hint: Choose firm eggplants that seem heavy for their size. They should have smooth, evenly colored skins free of scars or bruises.

FAT: 7G/21%
CALORIES: 307
SATURATED FAT: 3.5G
CARBOHYDRATE: 42G
PROTEIN: 23G
CHOLESTEROL: 67MG
SODIUM: 921MG

After years of stuffed turkey, chicken, pork chops, and the like, the idea of stuffed vegetables comes as a refreshing change. There are lots of ways to make them, and these attractive roll-ups present one of the easiest options. The blanched eggplant slices are rolled around a creamy spinach filling and then baked in a ruby-hued tomato sauce.

GREEK-STYLE STRATA

SERVES: 4
WORKING TIME: 15 MINUTES
TOTAL TIME: 50 MINUTES

A strata, as the name implies, is a layered dish. The time-honored American version is a stack of white bread and Cheddar, saturated with an eggy custard and baked. Our livelier (and much healthier) interpretation features whole-wheat pitas and flavorful feta cheese in a creamy low-fat custard studded with scallions, dill, and mint. Tomato slices make a bright topping.

3 whole-wheat pitas, cut into sixths
1 cup low-fat (1%) cottage cheese
1 cup low-fat (1%) milk
2 tablespoons flour
2 whole eggs
4 egg whites
3 ounces crumbled feta cheese
½ cup frozen peas
4 scallions, thinly sliced
½ cup snipped fresh dill
¼ cup chopped fresh mint
1 teaspoon grated lemon zest
⅛ teaspoon salt
¼ teaspoon freshly ground black pepper
1 tomato, thinly sliced

1. Preheat the oven to 350°. Toast the pitas until lightly crisp, about 5 minutes.

2. Meanwhile, in a food processor, process the cottage cheese and milk until smooth, about 1 minute. Transfer to a medium bowl and stir in the flour, whole eggs, egg whites, feta, peas, scallions, dill, mint, lemon zest, salt, and pepper. Place the pitas in an 11 x 7-inch glass baking dish and pour the egg mixture over. Let stand at room temperature for 10 minutes.

3. Spread the tomato slices over the top and bake for about 35 minutes, or until the custard is just set.

Helpful hint: The casserole can be assembled, covered, and refrigerated for up to 12 hours. Let it come to room temperature before baking.

FAT: 10G/26%
CALORIES: 349
SATURATED FAT: 4.9G
CARBOHYDRATE: 41G
PROTEIN: 26G
CHOLESTEROL: 130MG
SODIUM: 935MG

A *baked potato is the ideal starting point for a substantial meal, but be careful what you add to it: Lots of butter, sour cream, and bacon bits will make a high-fat meal out of the virtually fat-free potato. Our overstuffed spuds get their creamy richness from low-fat milk and cottage cheese. Corn, carrots, and scallions add a bit of crisp texture.*

Twice-Baked Potatoes

SERVES: 4
WORKING TIME: 10 MINUTES
TOTAL TIME: 1 HOUR 30 MINUTES

4 baking potatoes (about 8 ounces each)

¼ cup low-fat (1%) milk

1½ cups low-fat (1%) cottage cheese

¼ cup plus 2 tablespoons grated Parmesan cheese

⅔ cup frozen corn kernels, thawed

2 carrots, shredded

½ cup sliced scallions

½ teaspoon salt

¼ teaspoon freshly ground black pepper

1. Preheat the oven to 425°. Prick the potatoes in several places with a fork, place on a baking sheet, and bake for about 1 hour, or until fork-tender. Leave the oven on. When cool enough to handle, split the potatoes open (see tip) and scoop out the flesh, leaving a ¼-inch-thick shell.

2. Place the potato flesh in a medium bowl, stir in the milk, and mash. Stir in the cottage cheese, ¼ cup of the Parmesan, the corn, carrots, scallions, salt, and pepper, mixing until well combined. Spoon the potato mixture back into the potato shells, sprinkle with the remaining 2 tablespoons Parmesan, return to the oven, and bake for about 20 minutes, or until the filling is piping hot and and the top is lightly crusted. Divide the potatoes among 4 plates and serve.

Helpful hint: To save time, you can microwave the potatoes: Prick them in several places with a fork, then place in the microwave about 1 inch apart. Cook on high power for 15 to 20 minutes, then cover and let stand for 5 minutes.

FAT: 4G/11%
CALORIES: 317
SATURATED FAT: 2.2G
CARBOHYDRATE: 53G
PROTEIN: 19G
CHOLESTEROL: 10MG
SODIUM: 797MG

TIP

To break open the potatoes, using a fork, prick a cross in the top. Push from opposite ends of the potatoes to pop open the tops so you can easily scoop out the flesh.

Vegetarian Baked Beans

SERVES: 4
WORKING TIME: 20 MINUTES
TOTAL TIME: 50 MINUTES

Rich and savory dried mushrooms replace the usual salt pork here; molasses, mustard, and ginger ensure an old-fashioned flavor.

¼ cup dried mushrooms, such as shiitake or porcini
½ cup boiling water
1 tablespoon olive oil
1 onion, finely chopped
3 carrots, thinly sliced
5 cloves garlic, minced
Two 19-ounce cans white kidney beans (cannellini), rinsed and drained
1½ cups canned no-salt-added tomatoes, chopped with their juices
1 teaspoon grated orange zest
⅓ cup orange juice
3 tablespoons firmly packed dark brown sugar
2 tablespoons molasses
1 teaspoon ground ginger
1 teaspoon Dijon mustard
½ teaspoon salt

1. In a small bowl, combine the dried mushrooms and boiling water and let stand until softened, about 10 minutes. Remove the dried mushrooms from their soaking liquid, reserving the liquid. Rinse and coarsely chop the mushrooms. Strain the liquid through a paper towel-lined sieve and set aside.

2. Meanwhile, preheat the oven to 375°. In a large nonstick skillet, heat the oil until hot but not smoking over medium heat. Add the onion, carrots, and garlic and cook, stirring frequently, until the carrots are softened, about 7 minutes.

3. Transfer the vegetables to a 9-inch square glass baking dish and stir in the beans, tomatoes, orange zest, orange juice, brown sugar, molasses, ginger, mustard, salt, and the mushrooms and their soaking liquid. Cover and bake for about 20 minutes, or until the beans are richly flavored. Uncover and bake for 10 minutes, or until piping hot and bubbly.

Helpful hint: Shiitake are Japanese mushrooms, and porcini are Italian; you can substitute other imported dried mushrooms, which are sold in small plastic tubs in most supermarkets. These "generic" dried mushrooms are less expensive than shiitake or porcini.

FAT: 5G/12%
CALORIES: 383
SATURATED FAT: 0.6G
CARBOHYDRATE: 69G
PROTEIN: 17G
CHOLESTEROL: 0MG
SODIUM: 692MG

ON THE GRILL

4

orn, one of the focal points of Mexican cuisine, is partnered with zucchini and tomatoes in this meatless adaptation of a Mexican favorite. The vegetables are layered over a hearty tomato-basil paste and a low-fat cheese sauce, and are then topped with part-skim mozzarella. Heating the tostadas on a covered grill imparts a hint of smoky flavor.

ZUCCHINI AND CORN TOSTADAS

SERVES: 4
WORKING TIME: 25 MINUTES
TOTAL TIME: 25 MINUTES

½ cup low-fat (1%) cottage cheese

2 tablespoons nonfat cream cheese

¼ cup grated Parmesan cheese

¼ cup no-salt-added tomato paste

2 tablespoons chopped fresh basil

Eight 6-inch flour tortillas

2 cups frozen corn kernels, thawed

1 zucchini, coarsely grated

½ cup chopped scallions

4 plum tomatoes, thinly sliced

1 cup shredded part-skim mozzarella cheese (4 ounces)

1. In a blender or food processor, combine the cottage cheese, cream cheese, and Parmesan and process to a smooth purée. Set aside. In a small bowl, combine the tomato paste and basil.

2. Preheat the grill with a grill topper (see tip). Spray the grill topper—off the grill—with nonstick cooking spray. Place the tortillas on the grill topper and grill at medium, or 6 inches from the heat, turning once, for 1 minute, or until lightly browned and crisp.

3. Dividing evenly, spread the tortillas first with the tomato paste mixture, then the cottage cheese mixture, then with the corn, zucchini, scallions, tomato slices, and mozzarella. Return the tortillas to the grill topper, cover, and cook for 2 minutes, or until the cheese is melted and the topping is heated through. Divide the tostadas among 4 plates and serve.

Helpful hint: A grill topper is a flat sheet of metal perforated at regular intervals with small, round holes. It works much better than a regular wire grill rack when you're cooking delicate foods. If you don't have a grill topper, see the tip at right for how to make one from foil.

TIP

To make your own grill topper, tear off a large piece of heavy-duty foil and fold it in half to make a double layer. Using a two-tined fork, make a series of holes over the entire surface of the foil. Use the punctured foil to cover the grill rack—before preheating—and proceed as directed.

FAT: 10G/25%
CALORIES: 357
SATURATED FAT: 4.6G
CARBOHYDRATE: 49G
PROTEIN: 21G
CHOLESTEROL: 22MG
SODIUM: 585MG

Mushroom Kebabs

SERVES: 4
WORKING TIME: 30 MINUTES
TOTAL TIME: 45 MINUTES PLUS MARINATING TIME

When asked to choose the vegetable that's most like meat, most people would probably say, "mushrooms." We've stacked these skewers with both big button mushrooms and flat-capped shiitakes, which are even "meatier" tasting. Tomatoes, bell peppers, and chunks of red onion grill along with the mushrooms. The accompanying bulghur pilaf is a snap to make.

12 large button mushrooms, halved

8 large fresh shiitake mushrooms (8 ounces), stemmed and halved

24 cherry tomatoes

2 green bell peppers, cut into 8 pieces each

1 red onion, cut into 16 chunks

5 tablespoons fresh lemon juice

4 teaspoons olive oil

1 teaspoon sugar

¾ teaspoon salt

1½ cups bulghur (cracked wheat)

3 cups boiling water

½ cup reduced-sodium vegetable broth

3 tablespoons reduced-fat sour cream

¼ cup plus 2 tablespoons chopped fresh parsley

½ cup raisins

3 tablespoons sliced almonds

1. Alternately thread the button mushrooms, shiitake mushrooms, cherry tomatoes, bell peppers, and onion onto eight 10-inch skewers. In a large pan, combine 3 tablespoons of the lemon juice, the oil, sugar, and ¼ teaspoon of the salt. Place the skewers in the pan, turning to coat well, cover with plastic wrap, and set aside to marinate for at least 30 minutes or up to 12 hours in the refrigerator.

2. In a medium, heatproof bowl, combine the bulghur and boiling water. Let stand until tender, about 20 minutes. Drain the bulghur and return it to the bowl. Stir in the broth, sour cream, parsley, raisins, almonds, the remaining 2 tablespoons lemon juice, and remaining ½ teaspoon salt.

3. Meanwhile, preheat the grill. Spray the rack—off the grill—with nonstick cooking spray. Reserving the marinade, transfer the skewers to the grill and cover. Grill at medium, or 6 inches from the heat, turning once and basting with some of the reserved marinade, for 10 to 12 minutes, or until the vegetables are tender. Divide the bulghur mixture among 4 plates and serve the kebabs alongside.

Helpful hint: If you can't get fresh shiitakes, you can use button mushrooms instead.

FAT: 10G/22%
CALORIES: 412
SATURATED FAT: 1.8G
CARBOHYDRATE: 76G
PROTEIN: 14G
CHOLESTEROL: 4MG
SODIUM: 480MG

ajor cleanup is the usual aftermath of grilling: There are often stubborn burned bits that need to be scraped and scrubbed off the grill. When you cook in packets, on the other hand, the food never touches the grill. This Caribbean combination of black beans, sweet potatoes, onion, and tomatoes includes a surprise ingredient—banana.

CARIBBEAN GRILLED VEGETABLE PACKETS

SERVES: 4
WORKING TIME: 20 MINUTES
TOTAL TIME: 50 MINUTES

1 pound sweet potatoes, peeled and cut into ¼-inch-thick slices

19-ounce can black beans, rinsed and drained

1 banana, thinly sliced

2 tablespoons fresh lime juice

2 teaspoons sugar

½ teaspoon salt

1 yellow summer squash, thinly sliced

1 red onion, thickly sliced

2 tomatoes, thickly sliced

⅓ cup chili sauce

2 teaspoons olive oil

¼ teaspoon freshly ground black pepper

¾ cup shredded jalapeño jack cheese (3 ounces)

1. In a medium pot of boiling water, cook the sweet potatoes until firm-tender, about 7 minutes. Drain well. In a medium bowl, toss the potatoes gently with the beans, banana, lime juice, sugar, and salt.

2. Preheat the grill. Tear off four 24-inch lengths of heavy-duty foil, fold each in half to form a 12 x 18-inch rectangle, and spray with nonstick cooking spray. Spoon the potato mixture into the center of each sheet. Top with the squash, onion, and tomatoes. Drizzle the chili sauce and olive oil over and sprinkle with the pepper. Top with the cheese and seal the packets (see tip).

3. Place the packets on the grill, cover, and grill at medium, or 6 inches from the heat, for about 20 minutes, or until the vegetables are piping hot and the squash is tender. Divide the packets among 4 plates and serve.

Helpful hint: The chili sauce used here is not an exotic ingredient—it's the familiar spicy, tomato-based condiment sold in bottles next to the ketchup at the supermarket.

FAT: 11G/27%
CALORIES: 363
SATURATED FAT: 4.2G
CARBOHYDRATE: 55G
PROTEIN: 14G
CHOLESTEROL: 23MG
SODIUM: 957MG

TIP

Grilling packets should be made of double layers of heavy-duty foil to prevent tearing. To seal the packets, draw the short ends of the foil together; then roll the edges together, making a series of ½-inch folds. Leave the final fold up to act as a handle. Last, fold in or crimp the sides of the packet.

ASIAN-STYLE GRILLED VEGETABLE SALAD

SERVES: 4
WORKING TIME: 40 MINUTES
TOTAL TIME: 40 MINUTES PLUS MARINATING TIME

*1 small head Napa cabbage
(¾ pound), trimmed and
quartered lengthwise*

¼ cup reduced-sodium soy sauce

¼ cup chili sauce

*¼ cup reduced-sodium vegetable
broth*

3 tablespoons fresh lime juice

2 tablespoons grated fresh ginger

1 clove garlic, minced

*4 teaspoons dark Oriental sesame
oil*

*1 pound firm, low-fat tofu, cut
into 2 large pieces*

*½ pound asparagus, ends
trimmed*

*1 red bell pepper, cut into
quarters*

6 scallions, trimmed

8 ounces linguine

1. In a large pot of boiling water, cook the Napa cabbage for 1 minute to blanch. Drain well. In a large bowl, combine the soy sauce, chili sauce, broth, lime juice, ginger, garlic, and sesame oil, whisking until well blended. Add the blanched cabbage, tofu, asparagus, bell pepper, and scallions. Toss the vegetables in the marinade to coat thoroughly and refrigerate for at least 1 hour or up to 12 hours.

2. In a large pot of boiling water, cook the linguine until just tender. Drain well.

3. Meanwhile, preheat the grill (with a grill topper, if possible). Spray the rack (or grill topper)—off the grill—with nonstick cooking spray. Reserving the marinade, transfer the vegetables and tofu to the grill and cover. Grill at medium, or 6 inches from the heat, turning once and basting with some of the reserved marinade, for 10 to 12 minutes, or until the vegetables are crisp-tender. When they are cool enough to handle, cut the vegetables and tofu into bite-size pieces.

4. Transfer the remaining marinade to a bowl. Add the linguine, grilled vegetables, and tofu, tossing to combine. Divide among 4 plates and serve.

Helpful hint: Napa, a Chinese cabbage, comes in a compact oblong head. The leaves are a greenish-cream color with delicately frilled edges.

FAT: 5G/14%
CALORIES: 325
SATURATED FAT: 0.7G
CARBOHYDRATE: 57G
PROTEIN: 14G
CHOLESTEROL: 0MG
SODIUM: 951MG

You can practically see the vibrant flavors in this delectable warm pasta salad. Asparagus, Napa cabbage, bell pepper, scallions, and tofu, marinated in a pungent Asian-inspired sauce, are grilled and then tossed with linguine. The rest of the marinade—a lively blend of chili sauce, soy sauce, sesame oil, lime juice, ginger, and garlic—serves as the salad dressing.

VEGETABLE SHISH KEBABS

SERVES: 4
WORKING TIME: 30 MINUTES
TOTAL TIME: 55 MINUTES PLUS MARINATING TIME

The yogurt-based marinade that flavors these skewered vegetables is a long-standing Middle Eastern tradition: It's seasoned with garlic, mint, sesame oil, and cumin as well as lemon. When the grilling is done, the marinade is transformed into a tasty sauce to serve with the skewers and orzo pasta.

½ pound red potatoes, cut into 1-inch chunks
2 cloves garlic, peeled
1½ cups plain nonfat yogurt
3 tablespoons chopped fresh mint
2 tablespoons fresh lemon juice
1 tablespoon dark Oriental sesame oil
1 teaspoon ground cumin
½ teaspoon salt
¼ teaspoon freshly ground black pepper
1 yellow summer squash, cut into 1-inch pieces
1 zucchini, cut into 1-inch pieces
1 red bell pepper, cut into 1-inch squares
8 cherry tomatoes
8 button mushrooms
6 ounces orzo pasta

1. In a medium pot of boiling water, cook the potatoes until tender, 8 to 9 minutes. Add the garlic during the last 2 minutes of cooking time. Drain. Mince the garlic.

2. In a medium bowl, combine the garlic, yogurt, mint, lemon juice, sesame oil, cumin, salt, and black pepper. Measure out 1 cup of the yogurt mixture and refrigerate until serving time. Alternately thread the cooked potatoes, yellow squash, zucchini, bell pepper, tomatoes, and mushrooms onto eight 12-inch skewers. Place the skewers on a baking sheet and brush the vegetables with the remaining yogurt mixture, turning the skewers to ensure even coating. Cover and marinate for at least 30 minutes at room temperature or up to 4 hours in the refrigerator.

3. Preheat the grill. Spray the rack—off the grill—with nonstick cooking spray. Place the skewers on the grill and cover. Grill at medium, or 6 inches from the heat, turning once, for 10 to 12 minutes, or until the vegetables are crisp-tender. Meanwhile, in a medium pot of boiling water, cook the pasta until tender. Drain well. Serve the vegetable skewers with the reserved yogurt-sesame sauce and the orzo.

Helpful hint: If possible, use metal skewers rather than wood for cooking kebabs—they hold the food better, and the handles make it easier to grip and move the hot skewers.

FAT: 5G/14%
CALORIES: 320
SATURATED FAT: 0.8G
CARBOHYDRATE: 57G
PROTEIN: 14G
CHOLESTEROL: 2MG
SODIUM: 352MG

Grilled Vegetable Pitas

SERVES: 4
WORKING TIME: 20 MINUTES
TOTAL TIME: 45 MINUTES PLUS MARINATING TIME

Take a break from the burger-on-a-bun habit with these unique sandwiches. We grill up generous quantities of vegetables and pile them into pita pockets (warm the breads on the grill for a few minutes, if you like). Chick-peas are added to the vegetables, ensuring that the heartiest appetites are satisfied. Offer an icy pitcher of tea or lemonade with the sandwiches.

¾ pound small red potatoes, halved

½ cup reduced-sodium vegetable broth

1 tablespoon olive oil

2 cloves garlic, minced

2 tablespoons Dijon mustard

1 teaspoon dried thyme

½ teaspoon freshly ground black pepper

¼ teaspoon salt

2 red or yellow bell peppers, quartered

2 yellow summer squash or zucchini, cut lengthwise into 4 thick slices

1 red onion, cut into ¼-inch-thick-slices

¾ cup low-fat (1.5%) buttermilk

3 tablespoons reduced-fat mayonnaise

¼ cup snipped fresh dill

16-ounce can chick-peas, rinsed and drained

4 large pita breads, halved

1. In a large pot of boiling water, cook the potatoes until tender, 10 to 12 minutes. Drain, rinse under cold water to stop the cooking, and drain again.

2. Meanwhile, in a large sturdy plastic bag, combine the broth, oil, garlic, 1 tablespoon of the mustard, the thyme, ¼ teaspoon of the black pepper, and the salt. Add the cooked potatoes, bell peppers, squash, and red onion. Toss the vegetables in the marinade to coat thoroughly and reseal the bag, squeezing out the air. Refrigerate for at least 1 hour or up to 12 hours.

3. Preheat the grill (with a grill topper, if possible). Spray the rack (or grill topper)—off the grill—with nonstick cooking spray. Transfer the vegetables to the grill and cover. Grill at medium, or 6 inches from the heat, turning once, for 10 to 12 minutes, or until the vegetables are crisp-tender. When they are cool enough to handle, cut the vegetables into bite-size pieces.

4. In large bowl, combine the buttermilk, mayonnaise, dill, the remaining 1 tablespoon mustard, and remaining ¼ teaspoon black pepper. Add the grilled vegetables to the buttermilk dressing along with the chick-peas. Divide the pita breads among 4 plates or baskets. Spoon the vegetable mixture into the pita breads and serve.

FAT: 9G/18%
CALORIES: 447
SATURATED FAT: 1.5G
CARBOHYDRATE: 75G
PROTEIN: 15G
CHOLESTEROL: 3MG
SODIUM: 907MG

GRILLED VEGETABLES WITH GARLIC MAYONNAISE

SERVES: 4
WORKING TIME: 25 MINUTES
TOTAL TIME: 50 MINUTES

6 cloves garlic, peeled

1 pound large red potatoes, cut into 32 chunks (about 1 inch)

4 carrots, halved lengthwise and cut into 6 pieces each

¾ cup reduced-sodium vegetable broth

3 tablespoons fresh lemon juice

1 tablespoon olive oil

¾ teaspoon salt

1 fennel bulb, cut into 16 pieces

4 large button mushrooms, quartered

8 cherry tomatoes

4 ounces Italian bread, cut on the diagonal into 4 slices

¼ cup plain nonfat yogurt

2 tablespoons reduced-fat mayonnaise

1 tablespoon reduced-fat sour cream

1. In a large pot of boiling water, cook the garlic for 2 minutes to blanch. With a slotted spoon, remove the garlic and set aside. Add the potatoes to the pot and cook until firm-tender, about 8 minutes. Add the carrots during the last 4 minutes of cooking time. Drain well.

2. Preheat the grill. In a large bowl, combine the broth, 2 tablespoons of the lemon juice, the oil, and ½ teaspoon of the salt. Add the potatoes, carrots, fennel, mushrooms, and tomatoes, tossing to coat. Alternately thread the vegetables onto eight 10-inch skewers.

3. Spray the rack—off the grill—with nonstick cooking spray. Place the skewers on the grill and cover. Grill at medium, or 6 inches from the heat, turning once, for 10 to 12 minutes, or until the vegetables are lightly browned and tender. Grill the bread until lightly browned, about 30 seconds per side.

4. Meanwhile, in a medium bowl, use a fork to mash the blanched garlic with the remaining ¼ teaspoon salt until soft. Stir in the yogurt, mayonnaise, sour cream, and the remaining 1 tablespoon lemon juice. Serve the vegetables with the grilled bread and garlic mayonnaise.

Helpful hint: You can substitute 1 large onion, cut into 16 chunks, for the fennel, if you like.

FAT: 7G/20%
CALORIES: 314
SATURATED FAT: 1.3G
CARBOHYDRATE: 55G
PROTEIN: 9G
CHOLESTEROL: 2MG
SODIUM: 821MG

What's a big bowl of mayonnaise doing in a healthy recipe? Well, it's really a mixture of three creamy ingredients— mayonnaise, yogurt, and sour cream—all in their low-fat forms. The mashed garlic blended into the sauce has been blanched to tame its sharp flavor; longer cooking would further gentle the garlic's bite.

GRILLED VEGETABLE PASTA

SERVES: 4
WORKING TIME: 25 MINUTES
TOTAL TIME: 45 MINUTES PLUS MARINATING TIME

If you're lucky, you've had the opportunity to try a dish something like this in a restaurant. But if you're smart, you'll use our recipe to make it at home, where you can grill the vegetables precisely to your taste. Equally important, you'll know exactly how much olive oil (a mere tablespoon) is in the marinade; restaurant chefs can be a bit heavy-handed with the oil jug.

1 small butternut squash (about 1 pound), peeled, halved lengthwise, seeded, and cut into ½-inch-thick slices

½ cup reduced-sodium vegetable broth

1 tablespoon olive oil

2 teaspoons grated lemon zest

½ teaspoon dried thyme

½ teaspoon dried oregano

¾ teaspoon salt

⅛ teaspoon red pepper flakes

8 plum tomatoes, halved lengthwise

1 red onion, cut into ¼-inch-thick slices

8 ounces penne pasta

¼ cup chopped fresh basil

½ cup grated Parmesan cheese

1 tablespoon chopped fresh parsley (optional)

1. In a large pot of boiling water, cook the butternut squash until tender, 8 to 10 minutes. Drain, rinse under cold water to stop the cooking, and drain again.

2. In a large sturdy plastic bag, combine the broth, oil, lemon zest, thyme, oregano, salt, and red pepper flakes. Add the cooked butternut squash, the tomatoes, and onion. Toss the vegetables gently in the marinade to coat thoroughly and reseal the bag, squeezing out the air. Refrigerate for at least 1 hour or up to 12 hours.

3. Preheat the grill (with a grill topper, if possible). When ready to cook, spray the rack (or grill topper)—off the grill—with nonstick cooking spray. Meanwhile, in a large pot of boiling water, cook the pasta until tender. Drain well and transfer to a large bowl.

4. Reserving the marinade, transfer the vegetables to the grill and cover. Grill at medium, or 6 inches from the heat, turning once and basting with some of the reserved marinade, for 10 to 12 minutes, or until the vegetables are crisp-tender. When they are cool enough to handle, cut the vegetables into bite-size pieces. Add the grilled vegetables to the pasta along with the remaining marinade and the basil, tossing to coat. Divide among 4 plates, sprinkle the Parmesan and parsley over, and serve.

FAT: 8G/19%
CALORIES: 376
SATURATED FAT: 2.5G
CARBOHYDRATE: 64G
PROTEIN: 14G
CHOLESTEROL: 8MG
SODIUM: 651MG

CURRIED VEGETABLES WITH CHUTNEY CREAM

SERVES: 4
WORKING TIME: 40 MINUTES
TOTAL TIME: 55 MINUTES PLUS MARINATING TIME

A dinner that can be started in advance is a welcome idea in busy households. With this recipe, you can pre-cook the vegetables, start them marinating, and make the sauce ahead of time, leaving only the grilling and rice-cooking to be done at mealtime. If you have a bunch of fresh parsley or cilantro on hand, chop some and stir it into the rice.

1 pound small red potatoes, quartered

Half a head of cauliflower (14 ounces), cut into 8 chunks

2 red bell peppers, cut into 16 pieces each

2 zucchini, cut into 8 pieces each

¼ cup fresh lemon juice

2 tablespoons olive oil

2 teaspoons curry powder

1 teaspoon ground coriander

¾ teaspoon salt

1 cup long-grain rice

1 cup plain nonfat yogurt

3 tablespoons mango chutney

2 tablespoons reduced-fat sour cream

1. In a medium pot of boiling water, cook the potatoes until tender, about 5 minutes. With a slotted spoon, remove the potatoes. Add the cauliflower to the pot and cook for 3 minutes to blanch. Drain. In a large bowl, combine the potatoes, cauliflower, bell peppers, zucchini, 2 tablespoons of the lemon juice, the olive oil, 1½ teaspoons of the curry powder, the coriander, and ½ teaspoon of the salt. Marinate for at least 30 minutes at room temperature or up to 12 hours in the refrigerator.

2. In a medium saucepan, bring 2¼ cups of water to a boil. Add the rice and the remaining ¼ teaspoon salt, reduce to a simmer, cover, and cook until the rice is tender, about 17 minutes.

3. Meanwhile, preheat the grill. Alternately thread the vegetables onto eight 12-inch skewers. Spray the rack—off the grill—with nonstick cooking spray. Place the skewers on the grill and cover. Grill at medium, or 6 inches from the heat, turning once, for 10 to 12 minutes, or until the vegetables are crisp-tender.

4. In a small bowl, combine the yogurt, chutney, sour cream, the remaining 2 tablespoons lemon juice, and remaining ½ teaspoon curry powder. Serve the vegetables with the rice and chutney cream.

Helpful hint: Use a glass, ceramic, or stainless steel bowl when marinating foods in an acid mixture such as this citrus-based sauce.

FAT: 9G/18%
CALORIES: 455
SATURATED FAT: 1.6G
CARBOHYDRATE: 83G
PROTEIN: 13G
CHOLESTEROL: 4MG
SODIUM: 621MG

VEGETABLE AND BEAN QUESADILLAS

SERVES: 4
WORKING TIME: 20 MINUTES
TOTAL TIME: 30 MINUTES

Layered tortillas, beans, corn, cheese, and salsa transform traditional quesadillas into this satisfying (and healthy) main course.

19-ounce can black beans, rinsed and drained

4 scallions, thinly sliced

1 tablespoon fresh lime juice

¾ teaspoon chili powder

½ teaspoon ground cumin

¾ teaspoon ground coriander

Twelve 6-inch low-fat flour tortillas

2 cups frozen corn kernels, thawed

1 cup shredded Monterey jack cheese (4 ounces)

½ cup mild to medium-hot prepared salsa

1. Preheat the grill. In a small bowl, mash the beans with the scallions, lime juice, chili powder, cumin, and coriander. Spread the bean mixture on 8 of the tortillas.

2. Tear off four 24-inch lengths of heavy-duty foil, fold each in half to form a 12 x 18-inch rectangle, and spray with nonstick cooking spray. Place a bean-topped tortilla, topping-side up, in the center of each rectangle. Sprinkle half of the corn, cheese, and salsa over. Top with another bean-topped tortilla, topping-side up, and sprinkle the remaining corn, cheese, and salsa over. Top each with one of the remaining tortillas and seal the packets (see hint).

3. Place the packets on the grill, cover, and grill at medium, or 6 inches from the heat, for about 12 minutes, or until the cheese has melted and the tortillas are lightly crisped. Remove the quesadillas from their packets, divide among 4 plates, and serve.

Helpful hint: Grilling packets should be made of double layers of heavy-duty foil to prevent tearing. To seal the packets, draw the short ends of the foil together; then roll the edges together, making a series of ½-inch folds. Leave the final fold up to act as a handle. Last, fold in or crimp the sides of the packet.

FAT: 13G/25%
CALORIES: 476
SATURATED FAT: 5.1G
CARBOHYDRATE: 73G
PROTEIN: 21G
CHOLESTEROL: 30MG
SODIUM: 960MG

SALADS

INDONESIAN VEGETABLE SALAD

SERVES: 4
WORKING TIME: 20 MINUTES
TOTAL TIME: 20 MINUTES

O*ne of Indonesia's best known dishes is "gado-gado," a salad of blanched and raw vegetables attractively arranged on a big platter. What makes it extra-special is the chilied peanut sauce that's spooned over the vegetables. We've subtracted the oil and coconut milk from the sauce. Still nutty and tangy, with the bite of red pepper, it's now a far healthier dressing.*

1 pound all-purpose potatoes, peeled and cut into ½-inch cubes

¾ pound green beans

¼ cup reduced-sodium soy sauce

3 tablespoons fresh lime juice

3 tablespoons smooth peanut butter

2 teaspoons firmly packed dark brown sugar

2 cloves garlic, peeled

¼ teaspoon red pepper flakes

16 Boston lettuce leaves

2 cups bean sprouts

2 tomatoes, cut into 8 wedges each

1 cucumber, peeled, halved lengthwise, seeded, and thinly sliced

2 cups juice-packed canned pineapple chunks, drained

1. In a large pot of boiling water, cook the potatoes until tender, about 7 minutes. With a slotted spoon, remove the potatoes. Add the green beans to the boiling water and cook until crisp-tender, about 4 minutes. Drain.

2. Meanwhile, in a food processor, combine the soy sauce, lime juice, peanut butter, brown sugar, garlic, red pepper flakes, and ¼ cup of water. Process to a smooth purée.

3. Line 4 plates with the lettuce leaves. Top with the bean sprouts, tomatoes, cucumber, and pineapple. Spoon the potatoes and green beans on top, drizzle the peanut sauce over, and serve.

Helpful hint: To seed a cucumber, cut it in half lengthwise and use the tip of a spoon to scrape out the seeds.

FAT: 7G/20%
CALORIES: 311
SATURATED FAT: 1.1G
CARBOHYDRATE: 58G
PROTEIN: 11G
CHOLESTEROL: 0MG
SODIUM: 686MG

Pasta Marinara Salad

SERVES: 4
WORKING TIME: 15 MINUTES
TOTAL TIME: 20 MINUTES

Among the most beloved pasta toppings is marinara, a zesty tomato sauce. And here's the easiest marinara you'll ever make—an uncooked version with fresh tomatoes and basil that's puréed in the food processor. Along with the pasta, the sauce dresses crisp asparagus and snow peas, meaty kidney beans, and cubes of mozzarella.

3 cloves garlic, peeled
10 ounces spinach fusilli
1 pound asparagus, tough ends trimmed and cut on the diagonal into 1-inch lengths
½ pound snow peas, strings removed
1 pound tomatoes, quartered
½ cup packed fresh basil leaves
½ cup low-sodium tomato-vegetable juice
2 tablespoons balsamic vinegar
1 tablespoon olive oil
¾ teaspoon salt
19-ounce can red kidney beans, rinsed and drained
6 ounces part-skim mozzarella, cut into ½-inch cubes

1. In a large pot of boiling water, cook the garlic for 2 minutes to blanch. Remove with a slotted spoon. Add the fusilli to the water and cook until tender, adding the asparagus and snow peas during the last 1 minute of cooking time. Drain well.

2. Meanwhile, in a food processor, combine the tomatoes, basil, tomato-vegetable juice, vinegar, oil, salt, and blanched garlic and process to a smooth purée, about 30 seconds.

3. Transfer the dressing to a large bowl and add the kidney beans, mozzarella, pasta, asparagus, and snow peas. Toss well and serve at room temperature or chill for up to 8 hours.

Helpful hint: Spinach pasta, which is colored and flavored with spinach, is actually no more or less nutritious than regular pasta. You can substitute plain fusilli, if you like.

FAT: 13G/20%
CALORIES: 581
SATURATED FAT: 5.1G
CARBOHYDRATE: 86G
PROTEIN: 33G
CHOLESTEROL: 25MG
SODIUM: 841MG

MEXICAN SALAD WITH SALSA VINAIGRETTE

SERVES: 4
WORKING TIME: 15 MINUTES
TOTAL TIME: 25 MINUTES

*1 pound small red potatoes,
halved*

1½ cups peeled baby carrots

1 cup frozen corn kernels

*⅔ cup mild to medium-hot
prepared salsa*

*½ cup low-sodium tomato-
vegetable juice*

3 tablespoons fresh lime juice

1 tablespoon olive oil

*1 yellow or red bell pepper, cut
into ½-inch-wide strips*

1 cup radishes, thinly sliced

*19-ounce can black beans, rinsed
and drained*

*½ cup chopped fresh cilantro or
basil*

¾ cup diced avocado (6 ounces)

1. In a large pot of boiling water, cook the potatoes until firm-tender, about 10 minutes. Add the carrots and cook until the potatoes and carrots are tender, about 4 minutes. Add the corn and drain well.

2. Meanwhile, in a large bowl, combine the salsa, tomato-vegetable juice, lime juice, and oil. Add the potatoes, carrots, corn, bell pepper, radishes, black beans, and cilantro, tossing well to combine. Serve at room temperature or chill for up to 8 hours. To serve, divide the salad among 4 plates and sprinkle with the avocado.

Helpful hint: Prewashed peeled baby carrots, a wonderful convenience item, are sold in bags in most supermarkets. You can substitute thin regular carrots cut into 2-inch lengths, if you like.

Even with salsa's huge popularity, the idea of using it as a salad dressing may not have occurred to you. We've transformed the chunky tomato-chili sauce into a pourable dressing by adding tomato-vegetable juice, lime juice, and a little olive oil. The salad features some Mexican favorites, including avocado, black beans, corn, and cilantro.

FAT: 11G/28%
CALORIES: 354
SATURATED FAT: 1.6G
CARBOHYDRATE: 56G
PROTEIN: 10G
CHOLESTEROL: 0MG
SODIUM: 464MG

If
the combination of
leeks and potatoes
sounds familiar,
that's because those
vegetables are the main
ingredients of
vichyssoise, the world-
famous cream soup. In
a lighter vein, this
salad combines red
potatoes with blanched
leeks and asparagus in
a dilled mustard
vinaigrette. To make a
low-fat vinaigrette, we
substitute broth for
some of the oil.

POTATO, LEEK, AND ASPARAGUS SALAD

SERVES: 4
WORKING TIME: 15 MINUTES
TOTAL TIME: 25 MINUTES

1½ pounds red potatoes, cut into
1-inch chunks

¾ teaspoon salt

1¼ pounds asparagus, trimmed
and cut on the diagonal into
1-inch lengths

3 leeks, halved lengthwise and
cut into 1-inch pieces (see tip)

⅔ cup reduced-sodium vegetable
broth

2 tablespoons red wine vinegar

1 tablespoon Dijon mustard

1 tablespoon extra-virgin olive
oil

¼ cup snipped fresh dill

½ pound mushrooms, thinly
sliced

½ cup crumbled feta cheese
(2 ounces)

1. In a large pot of boiling water, cook the potatoes with ¼ teaspoon of the salt until tender, about 10 minutes. Add the asparagus and leeks during the last 2 minutes of cooking time. Drain well.

2. In a large bowl, combine the broth, vinegar, mustard, oil, and the remaining ½ teaspoon salt. Stir in the dill. Add the potatoes, asparagus, leeks, and mushrooms, tossing gently to coat. Spoon onto 4 plates, sprinkle with the feta, and serve at room temperature.

Helpful hint: If you can't get leeks, you can make this salad with 12 scallions, blanched for just 30 seconds and cut into 1-inch lengths.

FAT: 8G/24%
CALORIES: 306
SATURATED FAT: 2.7G
CARBOHYDRATE: 51G
PROTEIN: 11G
CHOLESTEROL: 13MG
SODIUM: 672MG

TIP

When a recipe calls for leeks to be sliced, first trim the root end and the dark green leaves, then cut the leeks as directed. Place the cut leeks in a bowl of tepid water, let them sit for 1 to 2 minutes, then lift the leeks out of the water, leaving any dirt and grit behind in the bowl. This is easier and faster than splitting and washing whole leeks before slicing them.

Bean and Potato Salad with Yogurt Dressing

SERVES: 4
WORKING TIME: 20 MINUTES
TOTAL TIME: 30 MINUTES

great American side dish, potato salad, has the potential to be a solidly satisfying entrée as well. Two kinds of beans—pinto and lima—supply a hefty helping of protein, while celery and red onion add crunch. It would be a shame to drown these tasty ingredients in mayonnaise, so we've devised a yogurt vinaigrette, instead.

10-ounce package frozen baby lima beans

1 pound red potatoes, cut into ½-inch chunks

¾ teaspoon salt

1 cup plain nonfat yogurt

¼ cup cider vinegar

1 tablespoon Dijon mustard

½ teaspoon freshly ground black pepper

½ cup snipped fresh dill

16-ounce can pinto beans, rinsed and drained

1 red onion, cut into ¼-inch dice

3 ribs celery, thinly sliced

4 cups torn romaine lettuce

1. In a large pot of boiling water, cook the lima beans and potatoes with ¼ teaspoon of the salt until the potatoes are tender, about 10 minutes. Drain.

2. In a large bowl, combine the yogurt, vinegar, mustard, pepper, and the remaining ½ teaspoon salt. Stir in the dill. Add the lima beans, potatoes, pinto beans, onion, and celery, tossing gently to coat. Serve at room temperature or chill for up to 8 hours. To serve, divide the lettuce among 4 plates and top with the salad mixture.

Helpful hint: You can substitute another mustard (but preferably a fairly spicy one) for the Dijon, if you like. Creole mustard, which has a touch of horseradish added, would work well.

FAT: 1G/3%
CALORIES: 321
SATURATED FAT: 0.1G
CARBOHYDRATE: 61G
PROTEIN: 17G
CHOLESTEROL: 1MG
SODIUM: 746MG

BLACK-EYED PEA AND MUSHROOM SALAD

SERVES: 4
WORKING TIME: 20 MINUTES
TOTAL TIME: 35 MINUTES

*T*his combination of rice and legumes is an abundant source of protein. Marinated mushrooms add plenty of flavor.

⅓ cup fresh lemon juice

⅓ cup reduced-sodium vegetable broth

⅓ cup red wine vinegar

3 tablespoons extra-virgin olive oil

1¼ teaspoons salt

¾ teaspoon freshly ground black pepper

½ teaspoon hot pepper sauce

½ pound button mushrooms, thickly sliced

¼ pound shiitake mushrooms, trimmed and thinly sliced

1 cup long-grain rice

10-ounce package frozen black-eyed peas

10-ounce package frozen green peas

4 scallions, thinly sliced

8 large lettuce leaves

1. In a medium bowl, combine the lemon juice, broth, vinegar, oil, ¼ teaspoon of the salt, the black pepper, and hot pepper sauce. Add the button and shiitake mushrooms, tossing to coat.

2. In a medium saucepan, bring 4 cups of water to a boil. Add the rice and ¼ teaspoon of the salt, reduce to a simmer, cover, and cook for 5 minutes. Add the black-eyed peas, cover, and simmer until the rice and black-eyed peas are tender, about 15 minutes. Add the green peas and cook until just heated through, about 30 seconds. (If any liquid remains, drain the rice mixture.)

3. Add the rice mixture to the bowl with the mushrooms. Stir in the scallions and the remaining ¾ teaspoon salt. Serve at room temperature or chill for up to 8 hours. To serve, place 2 lettuce leaves on each of 4 plates and top with the salad mixture.

Helpful hint: You can make the salad with ¾ pound button mushrooms instead of using both shiitakes and button mushrooms.

FAT: 12G/24%
CALORIES: 452
SATURATED FAT: 1.8G
CARBOHYDRATE: 73G
PROTEIN: 16G
CHOLESTEROL: 0MG
SODIUM: 817MG

MIDDLE EASTERN BULGHUR SALAD

SERVES: 4
WORKING TIME: 15 MINUTES
TOTAL TIME: 35 MINUTES

1½ cups bulghur (cracked wheat)

3 cups boiling water

½ cup fresh lemon juice

2 tablespoons extra-virgin olive oil

¾ teaspoon salt

½ teaspoon freshly ground black pepper

½ teaspoon ground allspice

5 scallions, thinly sliced

½ cup chopped fresh parsley

⅓ cup chopped fresh mint

19-ounce can red kidney beans, rinsed and drained

¾ pound plum tomatoes, cut into ½-inch slices

1 large cucumber, peeled, halved lengthwise, seeded, and cut into ½-inch cubes

1. In a medium bowl, combine the bulghur and boiling water. Let stand at room temperature until tender, about 30 minutes. Drain.

2. Meanwhile, in a large bowl, combine the lemon juice, oil, salt, pepper, and allspice. Add the scallions, parsley, and mint, stirring to combine. Add the beans, tomatoes, cucumber, and bulghur and stir well. Serve at room temperature or chill for up to 8 hours.

Helpful hint: This make-ahead dish could be the centerpiece for a Middle Eastern buffet. You might serve it with warm pita breads, chick-peas, and roasted vegetables.

FAT: 9G/21%
CALORIES: 381
SATURATED FAT: 1.2G
CARBOHYDRATE: 66G
PROTEIN: 15G
CHOLESTEROL: 0MG
SODIUM: 607MG

This is a variation on tabbouleh salad; we've cut down on the oil and added extra vegetables.

COUSCOUS SALAD

SERVES: 4
WORKING TIME: 20 MINUTES
TOTAL TIME: 30 MINUTES

Here's a novel pasta salad made with couscous—a Middle Eastern pasta that takes the form of tiny beads—instead of the traditional macaroni. The couscous is steeped with raisins and then combined with roasted bell pepper strips, parsley, cucumber, scallions and a light citrusy dressing. It's served on a bed of mixed greens and topped with crumbled feta cheese.

2 red bell peppers
2 yellow bell peppers
½ cup fresh lemon juice
2 tablespoons extra-virgin olive oil
1 teaspoon paprika
¾ teaspoon ground ginger
½ teaspoon salt
½ teaspoon freshly ground black pepper
1½ cups couscous
4 cups boiling water
¾ cup raisins
⅓ cup chopped fresh parsley
1 cucumber, peeled, halved lengthwise, seeded, and cut into ½-inch cubes
3 scallions, thinly sliced
4 cups watercress, tough stems removed
4 cups torn Boston lettuce
½ cup crumbled feta cheese (2 ounces)

1. Preheat the broiler. Cut off the 4 sides of each bell pepper and remove the ribs. Broil the bell peppers, cut-sides down, for about 10 minutes, or until the skin is blackened. When cool enough to handle, peel and cut into ½-inch-wide strips.

2. Meanwhile, in a medium bowl, combine the lemon juice, oil, paprika, ginger, salt, and black pepper. In another medium bowl, combine the couscous and boiling water. Add the raisins, cover, and let stand until the couscous is tender, about 5 minutes. Drain the couscous if any liquid remains.

3. Transfer the couscous and raisins to the bowl with the dressing. Add the roasted pepper strips, parsley, cucumber, and scallions, tossing to combine. Serve at room temperature or chill for up to 8 hours. To serve, place the watercress and Boston lettuce on 4 plates, top with the couscous mixture, and sprinkle with the feta.

Helpful hints: To seed a cucumber, cut it in half lengthwise and use the tip of a spoon to scrape out the seeds. You can substitute dried figs for the raisins: Plump 6 ounces of figs in boiling water for about 15 minutes, then drain and coarsely chop.

FAT: 11G/20%
CALORIES: 505
SATURATED FAT: 3.3G
CARBOHYDRATE: 91G
PROTEIN: 15G
CHOLESTEROL: 13MG
SODIUM: 471MG

PEAR, WATERCRESS, AND LENTIL SALAD

SERVES: 4
WORKING TIME: 15 MINUTES
TOTAL TIME: 50 MINUTES

A year-round delight, this lovely salad, with its pears, lentils, watercress, and goat cheese, poses sweet against earthy, tart against savory. In the dressing, pear nectar intensifies the fruit flavor and also replaces some of the oil. It's a perfect dish for both casual meals and entertaining. A loaf of French bread would be a fitting accompaniment.

1 cup reduced-sodium vegetable broth
1½ cups lentils, rinsed and picked over
2 carrots, halved lengthwise and thinly sliced
½ teaspoon salt
½ teaspoon dried tarragon
¼ teaspoon freshly ground black pepper
½ cup pear nectar
¼ cup fresh lime juice
1 tablespoon olive oil
1 tablespoon Dijon mustard
1 tablespoon mango chutney
½ cup diced red bell pepper
4 Bartlett or Bosc pears, peeled, cored, and thinly sliced
1 bunch of watercress, tough stems removed
1 cup crumbled goat cheese or feta cheese (4 ounces)
2 tablespoons coarsely chopped pecans

1. In a medium saucepan, bring the broth and 2 cups of water to a boil over medium heat. Add the lentils, carrots, salt, tarragon, and black pepper. Reduce to a simmer, cover, and cook until the lentils are firm-tender, about 25 minutes.

2. In a medium bowl, combine the pear nectar, lime juice, oil, mustard, and chutney. Add the lentil mixture, bell pepper, and pears, tossing until well coated.

3. Place the watercress on 4 plates, spoon the lentil mixture over, sprinkle with the goat cheese and pecans, and serve.

Helpful hint: The salad can be prepared ahead of time through step 2 and refrigerated for up to 8 hours.

FAT: 16G/25%
CALORIES: 568
SATURATED FAT: 6.6G
CARBOHYDRATE: 84G
PROTEIN: 29G
CHOLESTEROL: 22MG
SODIUM: 660MG

Italian Bread and Vegetable Salad

Serves: 4
Working time: 30 minutes
Total time: 40 minutes plus chilling time

The Tuscan dish panzanella—a rustic salad of bread, tomatoes, onions, and herbs—originated as a use for leftover bread. But we use a fresh loaf and toast the bread cubes under the broiler. We've devised an oil-free dressing based on puréed peppers; be sure to let the salad stand for at least an hour to let the bread and vegetables absorb the dressing.

7 ounces Italian bread, halved lengthwise

2 cloves garlic, peeled and halved

5 bell peppers, mixed colors, halved lengthwise and seeded

1 tablespoon olive oil

2 yellow summer squash, halved lengthwise and cut into 1-inch pieces

2 zucchini, halved lengthwise and cut into 1-inch pieces

¾ teaspoon salt

⅓ cup red wine vinegar

½ cup reduced-sodium vegetable broth

2 tablespoons no-salt-added tomato paste

⅓ cup chopped fresh basil

3 ounces part-skim mozzarella, cut into ½-inch cubes

1. Preheat the broiler. Broil the bread 6 inches from the heat until golden brown, about 30 seconds per side. When cool enough to handle, rub the toasted bread with the garlic. Cut the bread into 1-inch cubes, and transfer to a large bowl.

2. Place the bell pepper halves, cut-sides down, on the broiler rack. Broil the peppers 4 inches from the heat for 12 minutes, or until the skin is blackened. When the peppers are cool enough to handle, peel them and cut into 1-inch squares.

3. Meanwhile, in a large nonstick skillet, heat the oil until hot but not smoking over medium heat. Add the yellow squash, zucchini, and ¼ teaspoon of the salt and cook, stirring frequently, until crisp-tender, about 7 minutes. Transfer to the bowl with the bread, tossing to combine.

4. Place ½ cup of the cut-up peppers in a food processor along with the vinegar, broth, tomato paste, and the remaining ½ teaspoon salt and process until smooth. Add the pepper purée to the bowl, along with the remaining cut-up peppers, the basil, and mozzarella, tossing to combine. Refrigerate for at least 1 hour or up to 4 hours before dividing among 4 plates and serving.

Helpful hint: Either white or whole-wheat Italian bread is fine for this recipe.

Fat: 9g/28%
Calories: 289
Saturated Fat: 3.1g
Carbohydrate: 41g
Protein: 13g
Cholesterol: 12mg
Sodium: 803mg

PASTA-VEGETABLE SALAD WITH PESTO DRESSING

SERVES: 4
WORKING TIME: 30 MINUTES
TOTAL TIME: 30 MINUTES

6 cloves garlic, peeled

¾ pound fusilli

1½ cups packed fresh basil leaves

½ cup canned white kidney beans (cannellini), rinsed and drained

¼ cup grated Parmesan cheese

1 tablespoon olive oil

2 teaspoons pine nuts

½ teaspoon salt

2 red bell peppers, cut into ½-inch squares

½ pound mushrooms, thickly sliced

¾ pound asparagus, tough ends trimmed and cut on the diagonal into 1-inch lengths

6 Calamata or other brine-cured black olives, pitted and coarsely chopped

1. In a large pot of boiling water, cook the garlic for 2 minutes to blanch. With a slotted spoon, remove the garlic and set aside. Add the fusilli to the pot and cook until tender. Drain well and transfer to a large bowl.

2. Meanwhile, in a food processor, combine the garlic, basil, beans, Parmesan, 1 teaspoon of the oil, the pine nuts, and salt and process to a smooth purée. Add ⅓ cup of water and process until creamy. Pour the dressing over the pasta, tossing to combine.

3. In a large nonstick skillet, heat the remaining 2 teaspoons oil until hot but not smoking over medium heat. Add the bell peppers and cook, stirring frequently, until crisp-tender, about 4 minutes. Add the mushrooms and asparagus and cook, stirring frequently, until the asparagus is crisp-tender, about 4 minutes. Add to the bowl with the pasta. Add the olives, tossing to combine. Serve at room temperature or chill for up to 8 hours.

Helpful hint: Penne rigate (ridged penne) could be substituted for the fusilli; penne's shape, like that of fusilli, suits the other ingredients in the dish.

FAT: 10G/18%
CALORIES: 507
SATURATED FAT: 2.0G
CARBOHYDRATE: 87G
PROTEIN: 21G
CHOLESTEROL: 4MG
SODIUM: 561MG

If you're looking for a healthy pasta sauce, steer clear of the supermarket dairy case—the sauces found there are often loaded with fat. A commercial pesto sauce may have as much as 30 grams of fat in a quarter-cup serving! By comparison, our bean-based pesto, made with modest amounts of cheese, oil and pine nuts, is a minor miracle.

Mediterranean White Bean Salad

SERVES: 4
WORKING TIME: 20 MINUTES
TOTAL TIME: 25 MINUTES

Eggplant cooked with tomato paste and herbs takes on a robust, meaty flavor here that makes a pleasing contrast to the cannellini.

Two 19-ounce cans white kidney beans (cannellini), rinsed and drained

¾ cup chopped fresh basil

3 tablespoons balsamic vinegar

2 tablespoons olive oil

1 eggplant, cut into ½-inch cubes

1 cup reduced-sodium vegetable broth

3 tablespoons no-salt-added tomato paste

¾ teaspoon dried tarragon

½ teaspoon salt

1 green bell pepper, cut into ½-inch squares

1 yellow summer squash, halved lengthwise and cut into ½-inch slices

2 ribs celery, cut into ½-inch slices

2 cups cherry tomatoes, halved

4 ounces bread sticks

1. In a large bowl, gently stir together the beans, ¼ cup of the basil, the vinegar, and 4 teaspoons of the olive oil.

2. In a large nonstick skillet, heat the remaining 2 teaspoons oil until hot but not smoking over medium heat. Add the eggplant, stirring to coat. Cook, stirring frequently, until lightly golden, about 4 minutes. Add the broth, tomato paste, tarragon, and ¼ teaspoon of the salt and bring to a boil. Reduce to a simmer, cover, and cook until the eggplant is tender, about 5 minutes.

3. Transfer the eggplant mixture to the bowl with the beans, add the bell pepper, squash, and celery, tossing to combine. Add the tomatoes, the remaining ½ cup basil, and remaining ¼ teaspoon salt. Serve at room temperature or chill for up to 8 hours. Divide among 4 plates and serve with the bread sticks.

Helpful hint: Green or golden zucchini can be substituted for the yellow squash.

FAT: 12G/24%
CALORIES: 452
SATURATED FAT: 1.5G
CARBOHYDRATE: 69G
PROTEIN: 21G
CHOLESTEROL: 0MG
SODIUM: 891MG

PASTA SALAD WITH SUN-DRIED TOMATO VINAIGRETTE

SERVES: 4
WORKING TIME: 20 MINUTES
TOTAL TIME: 30 MINUTES

½ cup sun-dried (not oil-packed) tomatoes

1 cup boiling water

½ cup reduced-sodium vegetable broth

½ cup packed fresh basil leaves

¼ cup balsamic or red wine vinegar

tablespoons extra-virgin olive oil

¼ teaspoon salt

10-ounce package frozen Italian flat green beans

10 ounces medium pasta shells

4 cups cherry tomatoes, halved

9-ounce can chick-peas, rinsed and drained

1 red onion, cut into ¼-inch dice

1. In a small bowl, combine the sun-dried tomatoes and boiling water. Let stand at room temperature until softened, about 15 minutes. When softened, transfer the tomatoes and their soaking liquid to a food processor and process to a smooth purée, about 1 minute. Add the broth, basil, vinegar, oil, and salt and process until well combined. Transfer to a large bowl.

2. Meanwhile, in a large pot of boiling water, cook the green beans until crisp-tender, about 2 minutes. With a slotted spoon, transfer the beans to the bowl with the dressing; set aside. Add the pasta to the boiling water and cook until tender. Drain well and add to the bowl along with the cherry tomatoes, chick-peas, and onion, tossing to combine. Serve at room temperature or chill for up to 4 hours.

Helpful hint: If you can get fresh Italian flat green beans, use them in place of the frozen. The cooking time will be approximately the same, depending on the size of the fresh beans. Test them after 2 minutes and if they are still too raw, continue cooking them.

FAT: 11G/18%
CALORIES: 544
SATURATED FAT: 1.3G
CARBOHYDRATE: 94G
PROTEIN: 21G
CHOLESTEROL: 0MG
SODIUM: 352MG

Red, white, and green—the colors of the Italian flag—are fitting colors for this sensational Italian salad.

145

Apple and Plum Pasta Salad

Serves: 4
Working time: 25 minutes
Total time: 30 minutes

The apple slices, walnuts, and mayonnaise dressing reveal the inspiration for this dish: It's Waldorf salad, an American tradition since the 1890s. We've introduced pasta to the mix—bow ties seem appropriate to the formality of the Waldorf. The plums, red cabbage, and hard-cooked eggs are innovations, too; we've also lightened (and spiced up) the dressing.

8 ounces farfalle (bow ties) or rotini pasta

1½ cups plain nonfat yogurt

½ cup frozen apple juice concentrate, thawed

3 tablespoons reduced-fat mayonnaise

1 teaspoon ground ginger

½ teaspoon salt

2 cups shredded red cabbage

2 large red plums (6 ounces each), thinly sliced

1 McIntosh apple, halved, cored, and thinly sliced

1 Granny Smith apple, halved, cored, and thinly sliced

3 ribs celery, thinly sliced

2 hard-cooked eggs, peeled and coarsely chopped

2 tablespoons coarsely chopped walnuts

1. In a large pot of boiling water, cook the pasta until tender. Drain well.

2. In a large bowl, combine the yogurt, apple juice concentrate, mayonnaise, ginger, and salt. Add the pasta, cabbage, plums, apples, and celery, stirring to coat. Divide among 4 plates, sprinkle with the eggs and walnuts, and serve.

Helpful hints: We use two types of apples here, 1 red and 1 green. You can use all of one kind, if you like. Although we call for red plums, you can use almost any plum variety for this recipe. For perfect hard-cooked eggs, place the eggs in a small pot with cold water to cover. Bring to a boil, turn off the heat, cover, and let stand for 15 minutes. Peel the eggs under cold running water.

Fat: 9g/16%
Calories: 519
Saturated Fat: 1.7g
Carbohydrate: 94g
Protein: 18g
Cholesterol: 108mg
Sodium: 503mg

On Chinese restaurant menus, an all-vegetable stir-fry is sometimes called "Buddhist's Delight." We've come up with a salad-bowl version of the dish, replete with Chinese vegetables—Napa cabbage, snow peas, baby corn, and bamboo shoots—as well as tofu. The dressing is much like a tangy stir-fry sauce.

ORIENTAL VEGETABLE SALAD

SERVES: 4
WORKING TIME: 20 MINUTES
TOTAL TIME: 25 MINUTES PLUS CHILLING TIME

¼ cup rice vinegar

3 tablespoons reduced-sodium soy sauce

2 tablespoons ketchup

1 tablespoon dark Oriental sesame oil

1 tablespoon firmly packed dark brown sugar

¼ teaspoon salt

3 cups broccoli florets

6 ounces snow peas, strings removed

3 cups shredded Napa cabbage (see tip)

¼ pound mushrooms, thinly sliced

1 red bell pepper, cut into ½-inch-wide strips

2 cups canned baby corn, rinsed and drained

8-ounce can sliced bamboo shoots, drained

4 ounces firm low-fat tofu, cut into ¼-inch dice

1. In a large bowl, whisk together the vinegar, soy sauce, ketchup, sesame oil, brown sugar, and salt until well combined.

2. In a medium pot of boiling water, cook the broccoli for 2 minutes to blanch, adding the snow peas during the last 30 seconds of cooking time. Drain well, run under cold water to stop the cooking, and drain again.

3. Add the broccoli and snow peas to the bowl with the dressing, along with the cabbage, mushrooms, bell pepper, corn, and bamboo shoots. Toss well to combine, add the tofu, and toss gently. Refrigerate for at least 1 hour or up to 4 hours before dividing among 4 bowls and serving.

Helpful hint: If you have a hinged egg slicer, you can use it to slice mushrooms quickly. Buy large mushrooms and place them stemmed-side up in the slicer.

FAT: 6G/29%
CALORIES: 187
SATURATED FAT: 0.6G
CARBOHYDRATE: 27G
PROTEIN: 12G
CHOLESTEROL: 0MG
SODIUM: 760MG

TIP

To shred Napa cabbage, first remove each leaf individually. Stack 3 to 4 leaves at a time and, with a large chef's knife, trim off and discard the tough ends. Then cut the stacked leaves crosswise into thin shreds about ¼ inch wide.

BARLEY, CORN, AND PEPPER SALAD

SERVES: 4
WORKING TIME: 15 MINUTES
TOTAL TIME: 1 HOUR

This filling two-grain salad employs a neat trick to make cleanup easier: The brown rice and barley (as well as the carrots) are cooked in a single pot. The salad is tossed with a buttermilk-dill dressing that you'll want to try on other combinations of grains and vegetables, and on leafy greens, too. Serve the salad with squares of warm corn bread for a homey accompaniment.

2 cups reduced-sodium vegetable broth
2 carrots, halved lengthwise and thinly sliced
4 cloves garlic, minced
⅔ cup brown rice
¾ cup quick-cooking barley
1½ cups low-fat (1.5%) buttermilk
3 tablespoons reduced-fat sour cream
3 tablespoons fresh lemon juice
½ teaspoon salt
½ teaspoon freshly ground black pepper
¾ cup snipped fresh dill
1½ cups frozen corn kernels
1 red bell pepper, cut into ½-inch squares
¼ cup coarsely chopped cashews
16 Boston lettuce leaves

1. In a medium saucepan, combine the broth and 2 cups of water and bring to a boil over medium heat. Add the carrots, garlic, and rice; reduce to a simmer, cover, and cook for 20 minutes. Add the barley, return to a boil, reduce to a simmer, cover, and cook until the rice and barley are tender, about 15 minutes.

2. In a large bowl, combine the buttermilk, sour cream, lemon juice, salt, and black pepper. Stir in the dill. Add the corn, bell pepper, and cashews. Add the barley mixture, tossing well to combine. Serve at room temperature or chill for up to 8 hours. Divide the lettuce among 4 plates, spoon the salad over, and serve.

Helpful hint: The easiest way to prepare the dill is by snipping the leaves with kitchen shears. Snip the dill right into the measuring cup.

FAT: 9G/19%
CALORIES: 430
SATURATED FAT: 2.7G
CARBOHYDRATE: 77G
PROTEIN: 15G
CHOLESTEROL: 9MG
SODIUM: 480MG

MARINATED BEAN SALAD

SERVES: 4
WORKING TIME: 15 MINUTES
TOTAL TIME: 25 MINUTES

Get out the picnic basket and put this summery favorite at the top of the menu. Promoted from side-dish to main-dish status, this salad offers the luxurious accent of artichoke hearts, plus cherry tomatoes and Cheddar cheese. Try it as a sandwich filling, in sturdy French or Italian rolls lined with lettuce leaves—or simply serve the salad with good crusty bread.

½ cup red wine or balsamic vinegar

2 tablespoons fresh lemon juice

2½ teaspoons extra-virgin olive oil

2 teaspoons Dijon mustard

2 cloves garlic, minced

¼ teaspoon salt

19-ounce can chick-peas, rinsed and drained

19-ounce can red kidney beans, rinsed and drained

1 green bell pepper, cut into ½-inch squares

9-ounce package frozen artichoke hearts

½ pound green beans, cut into 1-inch lengths

2 cups cherry tomatoes, halved

2 ounces Cheddar cheese, cut into ¼-inch dice

1. In a medium bowl, combine the vinegar, lemon juice, oil, mustard, garlic, and salt. Add the chick-peas, kidney beans, and bell pepper. Let stand at room temperature while you prepare the remainder of the salad, or cover and refrigerate for several hours or up to 2 days before finishing the salad.

2. In a medium pot of boiling water, cook the artichoke hearts for 7 minutes. Add the green beans and cook until the green beans and artichokes are tender, about 4 minutes. Add to the bowl with the kidney beans, stir in the tomatoes and Cheddar, and serve at room temperature or chilled.

Helpful hint: Artichoke hearts canned in brine can be used instead of frozen artichokes; rinse and drain them before using (they don't need to be cooked). Don't substitute marinated artichoke hearts sold in jars, because they're packed in oil.

FAT: 11G/29%
CALORIES: 337
SATURATED FAT: 3.6G
CARBOHYDRATE: 43G
PROTEIN: 19G
CHOLESTEROL: 15MG
SODIUM: 638MG

GLOSSARY

Barley, pearl—Barley grain stripped of the husk and embryo, then steamed and polished, making it relatively quick cooking. This soup-making staple comes in three sizes: coarse, medium, and fine, plus a quick-cooking version (precooked by steaming) that's ready in 15 minutes rather than 55.

Basil—A highly fragrant herb with a flavor somewhere between licorice and cloves. Like many fresh herbs, basil will retain more of its taste if added at the end of cooking; dried basil is quite flavorful and can stand up to longer cooking. Store fresh basil by placing the stems in a container of water and covering the leaves loosely with a plastic bag.

Beans, black—Pea-sized oval black legumes much used in Latin American cuisine. Black beans, also called turtle beans, are fairly soft, with an earthy flavor. They come in both dried and canned (rehydrated, ready-to-use) forms. Black beans, like all canned beans, should be rinsed and drained before using to remove the high-sodium canning liquid and freshen the beans' flavor.

Bulghur—A form of cracked wheat that is pre-steamed, then dried and cracked so that it cooks quickly. The coarsest bulghur is used like rice, while the finest grain is used for the Middle Eastern grain salad called tabbouleh. Bulghur can be cooked on the stove, or steeped by pouring water over it.

Cayenne pepper—A hot spice ground from dried red chili peppers. Add cayenne to taste when preparing Mexican, Tex-Mex, Indian, Chinese, and Caribbean dishes; start with just a small amount, as cayenne is fiery hot.

Cheddar cheese—A semi-hard cow's milk cheese that can be mild or very sharp. It ranges in color from ivory to bright orange. Cheddar adds tangy richness to casseroles, soups, and salads, but should be used sparingly since it is high in fat. With strongly flavored sharp Cheddar, a little will go a long way. (Reduced-fat Cheddar will not melt as well.) Refrigerate, well wrapped, for up to 3 weeks.

Chili powder—A commercially prepared seasoning mixture made from ground dried chilies, oregano, cumin, coriander, salt, and dehydrated garlic, and sometimes cloves and allspice; used in chilis, sauces, and spice rubs for a Southwestern punch. Pure ground chili powder, without any added spices, is also available. Chili powders can range in strength from mild to very hot; for proper potency, use within 6 months of purchase.

Chili sauce—A thick, ketchup-like tomato sauce seasoned with chilies (or chili powder), garlic, and spices. Chili sauce is convenient, flavorful option for "spiking" Mexican, Tex-Mex, Creole, and other spicy-hot dishes. Nutritionally, chili sauce is roughly equivalent to ketchup, and can be substituted for ketchup if you like the heat.

Cilantro/Coriander—A lacy-leaved green herb (called by both names). The plant's seeds are dried and used as a spice (known as coriander). The fresh herb, much used in Mexican and Asian cooking, looks like pale flat-leaf parsley and is strongly aromatic. Store fresh cilantro by placing the stems in a container of water and covering the leaves loosely with a plastic bag. Coriander seeds are important in Mexican and Indian cuisines; sold whole or ground, they have a somewhat citrusy flavor that complements both sweet and savory dishes.

Cornstarch—A fine flour made from the germ of corn. Cornstarch, like flour, is used as a fat-free sauce thickener; cornstarch-thickened sauces are lighter, glossier, and more translucent than those made with flour. To prevent lumps, combine the cornstarch with a cold liquid before adding it to a hot sauce; bring it gently to a boil and don't stir too vigorously or the sauce may thin.

Cottage cheese—A tangy, spoonable cheese, available in creamed (highest in fat) and dry-curd styles. Low-fat versions of cottage cheese can be puréed to thick, "creamy," low-fat sauces. Cottage cheese is perishable and should be used within a week of purchase.

Cream cheese, reduced-fat—A light cream cheese, also called Neufchâtel, with about one-third less fat than regular cream cheese. It can be used as a substitute for regular cream cheese. A small amount used in sauces duplicates the richness of full-fat cream cheese or heavy cream.

Curry powder—Not one spice but a mix of spices, commonly used in Indian cooking to flavor a dish with sweet heat and add a characteristic yellow-orange color. While curry blends vary (consisting of as many as 20 herbs and spices), they typically include turmeric (for its vivid yellow color), fenugreek, ginger, cardamom, cloves, cumin, coriander, and cayenne pepper. Commercially available Madras curry is hotter than other store-bought types.

Dill—A name given to both the fresh herb and the small, hard seeds that are used as a spice. Add the light, lemony, fresh dill leaves (also called dillweed) toward the end of cooking. Dill seeds provide a pleasantly distinctive bitter taste and marry beautifully with sour cream- or yogurt-based dishes.

Eggplant—An oval-, pear-, or zucchini-shaped vegetable with deep purple or white skin and porous pale-green flesh.  Since the spongy flesh readily soaks up oil, it's better to bake, broil, or grill eggplant; the last two methods give this vegetable a deep, smoky flavor as well. Choose a firm, glossy, unblemished eggplant that seems heavy for its size. Don't buy eggplant too far in advance—it will turn bitter if kept too long. Store eggplant in the refrigerator for 3 to 4 days.

Evaporated milk, skimmed and low-fat—Canned, unsweetened, homogenized milk that has had most or all of its fat removed: In the skimmed version, 100 percent of the fat has been removed; the low-fat version contains 1 percent fat. Used in soups and sauces, these products add a creamy richness but almost no fat. Store at room temperature for up to 6 months until opened, then refrigerate for up to 1 week.

Feta cheese—A soft, crumbly, cured Greek cheese, traditionally made from sheep's or goat's milk. White and rindless, feta is usually available as a square block packed in brine; it's best to rinse it before using to eliminate some of the sodium. Use feta in casseroles and salads for bold flavor.

Garlic—The edible bulb of a plant closely related to onions, leeks, and chives. Garlic can be pungently assertive or sweetly mild, depending on how it is prepared: Minced or crushed garlic yields a more powerful flavor than whole or halved cloves. Whereas sautéing turns garlic rich and savory, slow simmering or roasting produces a mild, mellow flavor. Select firm, plump heads with dry skins; avoid heads that have begun to sprout. Store garlic in an open or loosely covered container in a cool, dark place for up to 2 months.

Ginger—A thin-skinned root used as a seasoning. Fresh ginger adds sweet pungency to Asian and Indian dishes. Tightly wrapped, unpeeled fresh ginger can be refrigerated for 1 week or frozen for up to 6 months. Ground ginger is not a true substitute for fresh, but it will lend a warming flavor to soups, stews, and sauces.

Goat cheese—A variety of cheeses made from goat's milk; often called by the French name, *chèvre*. You can choose from mild, spreadable types; firm, tangy ones; or assertive, well-aged *chèvres*. A fairly young cheese in log form is just the thing for general cooking purposes. (Small logs are sold whole, large ones by the slice.) Some examples are Montrachet, Chevrotin, Banon, Chabis, Ste. Maure, and Bucheron. Feta cheese is a reliable substitute in most recipes.

Lima beans—Large, flat, kidney-shaped beans, named for Lima, Peru. This bean comes in two varieties: the Fordhook and the baby lima, the latter being smaller and more delicate in flavor. Fresh limas, usually sold in their pods, are available during the summer months; the frozen can always be substituted. Limas work well in sautés, casseroles, soups, or even with pasta, providing a meaty texture as well as protein.

Monterey jack cheese—A mild cheese made from whole or skim milk, originally produced in Monterey, California. It has a delicate flavor, similar to American Muenster. The cheese melts readily and, shredded into a casserole, gives a milky richness. Often used in Southwestern cooking to "cool" the heat of chili peppers.

Mozzarella cheese—A very mild-flavored Italian cheese with exceptional melting properties. Mozzarella was originally made from water buffalo's milk, but is now more commonly made from cow's milk; it is available in whole-milk, part-skim, and fat-free varieties. The part-skim variety is the best option for cooking, as it is relatively low in fat but still has a nice texture and good melting properties. The rubbery texture of nonfat mozzarella makes it unsuitable for most recipes.

Olive oil—A fragrant oil pressed from olives. Olive oil is one of the signature ingredients of Italian cuisine. This oil is rich in monounsaturated fats, which make it more healthful than butter and other solid shortenings. Olive oil comes in different grades, reflecting the method used to refine the oil and the resulting level of acidity. The finest, most expensive oil is cold-pressed extra-virgin, which should be reserved for flavoring salad dressings and other uncooked or lightly cooked foods. Virgin and pure olive oils are slightly more acidic with less olive flavor, and are fine for most types of cooking.

Oregano—A member of the mint family characterized by small, green leaves. Prized for its pleasantly bitter taste, oregano is an essential ingredient in many Mediterranean-style dishes and is used in Mexican cooking as well.

Paprika—A spice ground from a variety of dried red peppers and used in many traditional Hungarian and Spanish dishes. Paprika colors foods a characteristic brick-red and flavors dishes from sweet to spicy-hot, depending on the pepper potency. Like all pepper-based spices, paprika loses its color and flavor with time; check your supply and replace it if necessary.

Parmesan cheese—An intensely flavored, hard grating cheese. Genuine Italian Parmesan, stamped "Parmigiano-

Reggiano" on the rind, is produced in the Emilia-Romagna region, and tastes richly nutty with a slight sweetness. Buy Parmesan in blocks and grate it as needed for best flavor and freshness. For a fine, fluffy texture that melts into hot foods, grate the cheese in a hand-cranked grater.

Parsley—A popular herb available in two varieties. Curly parsley, with lacy, frilly leaves, is quite mild and is preferred for garnishing, while flat-leaf Italian parsley has a stronger flavor and is better for cooking. Store parsley as you would basil. Since fresh parsley is so widely available, there is really no reason to use dried, which has very little flavor.

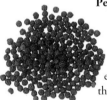

Pepper, black—The dried berries of a tropical vine, *piper nigrum.* This hot, pungent seasoning is sold in ground form and as whole berries, called peppercorns. A touch of pepper enlivens just about any savory dish, and the flavor of freshly ground pepper is so vastly superior to pre-ground that no good cook should be without a pepper grinder filled with peppercorns.

Red pepper flakes—A spice made from a variety of dried red chili peppers. Pepper flakes will permeate a stew or a casserole with a burst of heat and flavor during the cooking and eating. Begin with a small amount—you can always add more.

Rice, long-grain—A type of rice with grains much longer than they are wide. Long-grain rice remains fluffy and separate when cooked. Converted rice, which has been specially processed to preserve nutrients, takes slightly longer to cook than regular white rice. Rice is ideal for low-fat cooking since it absorbs other flavors and is quite filling, yet it contributes almost no fat; it's the perfect companion for stir-fries and curried dishes.

Ricotta cheese—A fresh, creamy white, Italian cheese with a grainier texture than cottage cheese and a slightly sweet flavor. Available in whole-milk and part-skim versions, it is often used in stuffed and baked pastas, and a little part-skim ricotta can be stirred into a sauce for added richness as well as creamy body.

Sesame oil, Oriental—A dark, polyunsaturated oil, pressed from toasted sesame seeds, used as a flavor enhancer in many Asian and Indian dishes. Do not confuse the Oriental oil with its lighter colored counterpart, which is cold-pressed from untoasted sesame seeds and imparts a much milder flavor. Store either version in the refrigerator for up to 6 months.

Sour cream—A soured dairy product, resulting from treating sweet cream with a lactic acid culture. Regular sour cream contains at least 18 percent milk fat by volume; reduced-fat sour cream contains 4 percent fat; nonfat sour cream is, of course, fat-free. In cooking, the reduced-fat version can be substituted for regular sour cream; use the nonfat cautiously since it behaves differently, especially in baking. To avoid curdling, do not subject sour cream to high heat.

Thyme—A lemony-tasting member of the mint family frequently paired with bay leaves in Mediterranean-style dishes and rice-based preparations. The dried herb, both ground and leaf, is an excellent substitute for the fresh.

Tofu—A soft, creamy white soybean product that is high in protein. A staple of most Asian cuisines, tofu (also called bean curd) can be sliced or cubed for use in soups, stews, stir-fries, and sautés; since its flavor is neutral, it works with many ingredients and seasonings. For the recipes in this book, use firm tofu, which looks like little pillows, rather than soft tofu, which comes in straight-edged blocks; soft tofu would crumble apart if cooked in liquid. For freshness, purchase packaged, vacuum-sealed tofu. Once opened, immerse in fresh, cold water, cover tightly, and refrigerate: Use within 5 days, changing the water daily.

Watercress—A slightly peppery-tasting aquatic herb used to add zip to salads and cooked dishes. The assertive flavor of watercress provides a peppery counterpoint to savory or sweet flavors. To prepare, rinse under cold water and blot dry with paper towels. Remove the tough stem ends or, for a more delicate flavor, use just the leaves.

Yogurt, nonfat and low-fat—Delicately tart cultured milk products made from low-fat or skim milk. Plain yogurt makes a healthful base for marinades, sauces, and salad dressings.

Zest, citrus—The thin, outermost colored part of the rind of citrus fruits that contains strongly flavored oils. Zest imparts an intense flavor that heightens the impact of savory dishes. Remove the zest with a grater, citrus zester, or vegetable peeler; be careful to remove only the colored layer, not the bitter white pith.

Zucchini—A delicately flavored summer squash that looks like a cucumber with a speckled skin. The golden version of this squash makes a nice change: Its flesh is more yellow than that of regular zucchini, but the flavor is about the same.

Index

TIME-LIFE BOOKS

Time-Life Books is a division of Time Life Inc.

TIME LIFE INC.

PRESIDENT and CEO: George Artandi

TIME-LIFE BOOKS

PRESIDENT: John D. Hall
PUBLISHER/MANAGING EDITOR: Neil Kagan

GREAT TASTE-LOW FAT
Meatless Main Dishes

DEPUTY EDITOR: Marion Ferguson Briggs
MARKETING DIRECTOR: Cheryl D. Eklind

Consulting Editor: Catherine Boland Hackett

Vice President, Director of Finance: Christopher Hearing
Vice President, Book Production: Marjann Caldwell
Director of Operations: Eileen Bradley
Director of Photography and Research: John Conrad Weiser
Director of Editorial Administration: Judith W. Shanks
Production Manager: Marlene Zack
Quality Assurance Manager: James King
Library: Louise D. Forstall

Design for Great Taste-Low Fat by David Fridberg of
Miles Fridberg Molinaroli, Inc.

REBUS, INC.
PUBLISHER: Rodney M. Friedman
EDITORIAL DIRECTOR: Charles L. Mee

Editorial Staff for *Meatless Main Dishes*
Director, Recipe Development and Photography: Grace Young
Editorial Director: Kate Slate
Senior Recipe Developer: Sandra Rose Gluck
Recipe Developers: Helen Jones, Paul Piccuito
Writer: Bonnie J. Slotnick
Managing Editor: Julee Binder Shapiro
Editorial Assistant: James W. Brown, Jr.
Nutritionists: Hill Nutrition Associates

Art Director: Timothy Jeffs
Photographer: Lisa Koenig
Photographer's Assistants: Alix Berenberg, Katie Bleacher Everard,
    Rainer Fehringer, Petra Liebetanz
Food Stylists: Karen Tack, Karen Pickus
Assistant Food Stylists: Charles Davis, Ellie Ritt
Prop Stylist: Debrah Donahue
Prop Coordinator: Karin Martin

Library of Congress Cataloging-in-Publication Data

Meatless main dishes.
    p.   cm. -- (Great taste, low fat)
Includes index.
ISBN 0-7835-4562-2
1. Vegetarian cookery. 2. Low-fat diet--Recipes. 3. Quick and easy
cookery. I. Time-Life Books. II. Series.
TX837.M479   1996
641.5'636--dc20   96-33475
                                                           CIP

OTHER PUBLICATIONS

COOKING
WEIGHT WATCHERS® SMART CHOICE RECIPE COLLECTION
WILLIAMS-SONOMA KITCHEN LIBRARY

DO IT YOURSELF
THE TIME-LIFE COMPLETE GARDENER
HOME REPAIR AND IMPROVEMENT
THE ART OF WOODWORKING
FIX IT YOURSELF

TIME-LIFE KIDS
FAMILY TIME BIBLE STORIES
LIBRARY OF FIRST QUESTIONS AND ANSWERS
A CHILD'S FIRST LIBRARY OF LEARNING
I LOVE MATH
NATURE COMPANY DISCOVERIES
UNDERSTANDING SCIENCE & NATURE

HISTORY
THE AMERICAN STORY
VOICES OF THE CIVIL WAR
THE AMERICAN INDIANS
LOST CIVILIZATIONS
MYSTERIES OF THE UNKNOWN
TIME FRAME
THE CIVIL WAR
CULTURAL ATLAS

SCIENCE/NATURE
VOYAGE THROUGH THE UNIVERSE

*For information on and a full description of any of the Time-Life Books series
listed above, please call 1-800-621-7026 or write:*
Reader Information
Time-Life Customer Service
P.O. Box C-32068
Richmond, Virginia 23261-2068

METRIC CONVERSION CHARTS

VOLUME EQUIVALENTS
(fluid ounces/milliliters and liters)

US	Metric
1 tsp	5 ml
1 tbsp (½ fl oz)	15 ml
¼ cup (2 fl oz)	60 ml
⅓ cup	80 ml
½ cup (4 fl oz)	120 ml
⅔ cup	160 ml
¾ cup (6 fl oz)	180 ml
1 cup (8 fl oz)	240 ml
1 qt (32 fl oz)	950 ml
1 qt + 3 tbsps	1 L
1 gal (128 fl oz)	4 L

Conversion formula
Fluid ounces X 30 = milliliters
1000 milliliters = 1 liter

WEIGHT EQUIVALENTS
(ounces and pounds/grams and kilograms)

US	Metric
¼ oz	7 g
½ oz	15 g
¾ oz	20 g
1 oz	30 g
8 oz (½ lb)	225 g
12 oz (¾ lb)	340 g
16 oz (1 lb)	455 g
35 oz (2.2 lbs)	1 kg

Conversion formula
Ounces X 28.35 = grams
1000 grams = 1 kilogram

LINEAR EQUIVALENTS
(inches and feet/centimeters and meters)

US	Metric
¼ in	.75 cm
½ in	1.5 cm
¾ in	2 cm
1 in	2.5 cm
6 in	15 cm
12 in (1 ft)	30 cm
39 in	1 m

Conversion formula
Inches X 2.54 = centimeters
100 centimeters = 1 meter

TEMPERATURE EQUIVALENTS
(Fahrenheit/Celsius)

US	Metric
0° (freezer temperature)	-18°
32° (water freezes)	0°
98.6°	37°
180° (water simmers*)	82°
212° (water boils*)	100°
250° (low oven)	120°
350° (moderate oven)	175°
425° (hot oven)	220°
500° (very hot oven)	260°

*at sea level

Conversion formula
Degrees Fahrenheit minus
32 ÷ 1.8 = degrees Celsius